George C. Marshall,
Reporting for Duty
In the U.S. Army (1902-1945)

Mary Sutton Skutt
Blue Valley Books
Lexington, Virginia

ISBN 0-9661582-2-9
Library of Congress Card Number 2001117035

Published by Blue Valley Books
          107 Paxton Street
          Lexington, VA 24450

Other books by Mary Sutton Skutt
  Growing Up, By George! George C. Marshall's early years (1880-1901)

Photographs and maps courtesy of the George C. Marshall Research
Library Archives

Cover by Jeanne Pedersen, Director of Publications, George C.
Marshall Foundation

Printed by the News-Gazette Print Shop
Lexington, Virginia

George C. Marshall, Reporting for Duty is dedicated to my grandchildren, and to all students, who might gain some insight into the personality, character, and the dedication to duty of George C. Marshall. Today, true and dependable heroes are not easy to find. General Marshall is one we can all be proud to claim.

Mary Sutton Skutt

George C. Marshall, Reporting for Duty

In the U.S. Army (1902-1945)

Who in the World Was George C. Marshall?

June 26, 2001 was the 100th anniversary of George C. Marshall's graduation from the Virginia Military Institute in Lexington, Virginia, and VMI claims Marshall as its most famous graduate. So that students, their families, and others will know of him, a handsome bronze statute of General Marshall overlooks the VMI parade ground. It stands across the street from the Barracks and the Marshall Arch, through which cadets pass as they go about their daily routines. Across the parade ground from the statue is the George C. Marshall Foundation which houses the George C. Marshall Museum and the Marshall Research Library.

George C. Marshall's name is familiar at his alma mater, but his personal history is less well known. This author hopes this book of facts and anecdotes about his army career will help correct that situation. *George C. Marshall, Reporting for Duty* is a sequel to *Growing Up, By George!*, the story of Marshall's early years and four years at VMI, written and published by the author in 1997.

Born December 31, 1880, George Catlett Marshall, Jr. spent his childhood in Uniontown, Pennsylvania. As a young boy, Marshall was not a good student and disliked school, but he was bright and he loved history. He lived a small-town, family-centered, ordinary, life until he went to VMI. There, for the next four years he lived in another small-town, and as a member of the VMI family. While there, he decided to try the extra-ordinary life of the army as a profession.

George C. Marshall gave willingly of his talents with a constant and incredible sense of duty. After leaving military life, he served as secretary of state and was the vital force behind the creation of the European Recovery Plan, known worldwide as the Marshall Plan. In 1953, in recognition of that relentless effort, he became America's first professional soldier to win the Nobel Prize for Peace.

All Americans, and friends of Americans, should be grateful that when George C. Marshall left VMI in 1901, he was eager to begin *Reporting for Duty* in the U.S. Army.

Mary Sutton Skutt
August 2001

Dr. Larry I. Bland is the Editor of the Marshall Papers at the George C. Marshall Foundation in Lexington, Virginia and the number one source of information on General Marshall's life. When I asked how to tell students in grades 6-9 that George C. Marshall was not a warmonger, or interested in gathering medals, gaining personal power, prestige, or fame Dr. Bland said:

"We can learn a great deal from George Marshall's career, because it shows that even as a child "underachiever, "one can — through ambition, dedication, hard work, and personal integrity — reach a high level professionally. Fortunately for America, General Marshall reached this peak of experience and good judgment just as World War II was breaking out. Four generations of school children have been influenced by what has happened to the United States as a result of that war."

George Marshall, Jr., age 16 at home Uniontown, Pennsylvania

Reporting for Duty

Chapter 1

Look Out, Here Comes Marshall!

September 1897 — June 1901

George Marshall overheard his brother Stuart telling their mother that if George went to Virginia Military Institute he would surely "disgrace the family name." Hearing that comment made George determined to prove his brother wrong. George was not an A-type student, did not care much for school, and did not like to study. His brother figured George would fail. George decided he would not.

When he entered VMI in Lexington, Virginia on September 11, 1897, George Marshall was skinny, somewhat shy, and only sixteen. He took with him a note from his father to Superintendent Shipp. It said: "I send you my youngest and last. He is bright, full of life, and I believe he will do very well."

At that time, a college education was not common, and it was expensive. The cost to attend VMI was about four hundred dollars a year. George Marshall 's parents paid his expenses, including a spending allowance of about three dollars a month, and hoped for the best. They hoped he would earn high grades, like his older brother, and return to his hometown to become a successful businessman. That was not what George Marshall, Jr. wanted, and he soon made other plans.

He enjoyed learning, in his own way, but making high grades in all subjects was impossible for him. He took the assigned first-year courses of English, French, Drawing, and Mathematics that he passed with average grades. Starting in a class of 122 freshmen, his grades improved each year, and he stayed near the middle of his class. Although more than two thirds of his class left VMI without graduating, George Marshall finished fifteenth in his senior class of thirty-three and fifth in his major field of civil engineering. He did not fail, and he certainly did not disgrace his family 's name!

Achievement in the classroom was one way to succeed at VMI, but George Marshall found another route. All Fourth Classmen, (freshmen) had to suffer through the Rat Line, as the VMI first year initiation period is called, and George Marshall did that reasonably well, once he learned the system.

He discovered that he could play the VMI game better than most cadets could and became intent on winning it. He learned military techniques and routines, followed orders and rules without question, and polished his shoes until they shone like patent leather. In fact, the Superintendent questioned George because he had such shiny shoes! At the end of his first year, and each of his following years, he was first in the military rankings of his class.

During his second year, Marshall was the First Corporal, and in his third year, he was First Sergeant. He was often responsible for helping enforce daily discipline around the Post or in the Barracks. Whenever he was the O.D. (Officer of the Day), his duty was to "sock" (report) anyone he saw breaking any rules. It did not matter if the cadet was a freshman or a senior, his friend or not, if Marshall caught him, Marshall would report him. In his senior year, he was the highest ranking cadet in the corps, the First Captain.

At home in Pennsylvania, his nickname had been Flicker, perhaps because of the reddish color of his hair. At VMI, they called him Pug because of the shape of his nose. Pug Marshall was friendly, although a bit aloof and cool. The cadets knew he was fair-minded and had sharp eyes, so they were careful when he was on duty. Before he rounded the corner, one might hear, "Watch out for Pug!" or "Look out! Here comes Marshall."

Marshall's appointment as First Captain came as a reward for his self-discipline, integrity, and a natural ability to manage men. Henry Fry, editor of the 1901 VMI year book, said of George Marshall: " . . . with all his military efficiency he was very popular and well-liked, (with a) friendly disposition, he was a booster . . . never an unkind word about anybody . . . he put in the best he had."

During the summer of 1899, following his second college year, Marshall was home from VMI on vacation. He attended a welcome-home parade in Uniontown given for the 10th Pennsylvania Volunteer Infantry, who were returning from their adventures in the

Philippine Islands and the Spanish-American War. The streets were even painted red, white, and blue!

Almost forty years later, during another Uniontown celebration, one given in his honor, General Marshall gave a speech. In it, he said, "I have sometimes thought that the impression of that period, and particularly of that parade, had a determining effect on my choice of a profession . . . It was a grand American small town demonstration of pride in its young men and of wholesome enthusiasm over their achievements. Years later most of us realized it was much more than that. It reflected the introduction of America into the affairs of the world beyond the seas."

By the time he left VMI, Marshall certainly looked and acted the part of an officer. He was six feet tall, and carried himself in a dignified and authoritative manner. His stern voice commanded attention. When he gave orders on the parade ground, his voice carried loudly from one end to the other. Forrest C. Pogue, General Marshall's official biographer, wrote, "Marshall had applied himself diligently at VMI and acquired focus, skill, and self-confidence. But to become a general he needed in addition the chance to become a second lieutenant."

In order to get that chance, George had to apply and be selected then take and pass the tests given by the War Department. Had Marshall attended the U.S. Military Academy at West Point, he would not have had to take the tests, since West Point cadets were already in the Army. Only civilians were required to take the tests, and the competition was strong. He could have enlisted in the army as a private, but he wanted an officer's commission. He had to take the tests.

The year 1901 was a good time to be trying for a commission. The Spanish-American War had recently ended. The army was being enlarged, and there was a need for more lieutenants. However, there were 10,000 applications on file in the office of the War Department, and only 142 vacancies. George wanted a chance to take the tests and he made plans to get one. When his father knew there was no changing George's mind, he did what he could to help him. He contacted his influential friends working in and around Washington.

George C. Marshall, VMI senior, 1901   (Miley photo)

In April, George Marshall went, on his own, to Washington, D.C. to obtain permission from the War Department officials to take the tests. He collected letters that his father's friends had written . General Shipp had also written to President William McKinley. His letter said: "I assert with absolute confidence that if commissioned in the army, young Marshall will in all respects, soon stand much above the average West Point graduate."

Armed with the letters from his father's friends, he went to the White House to see President William McKinley. Although he had no appointment, Marshall was able to get into the President's office where he made his request in person.

As he told Forrest C. Pogue many years later, "Mr. McKinley, in a very nice way, asked what I wanted and I stated my case. I don't recall exactly what I said." Maybe President McKinley had nothing to do with it, but Marshall's name was on the list in mid-June of those selected to take the examination. The tests were scheduled for September.

George was pleased, but his family felt otherwise. They were concerned for his future. An army officer did not earn much money, and the job held no social prestige. But, George was determined. He did not want to be a businessman along with his father and brother. His profession would be in the U.S. Army. That is, if he passed the tests!

Virginia Military Institute's instructors and leaders may have given George Marshall some extra encouragement and direction, but it was his own idea and ambition to become an officer. George was one of the few cadets in his class who chose the Army for his career.

June 26, 1901, George Marshall's graduation day, was a dreary Wednesday with misty drizzle off and on all morning. For him, the weather probably did not make much difference. Even if leaving the safe territory of college life caused a chill of uncertainty to cross his mind, it didn't last for long. George Marshall was not facing the future alone. A ray of sunshine for him, on any day, was his sweetheart, Elizabeth Carter ("Lily") Coles, who had recently agreed to marry him. He had proposed, and she had accepted, but they could make no firm wedding plans until he received his commission.

Left tackle, George Marshall
VMI football 1900

First Captain Marshall,
VMI 1901

Elizabeth Carter Coles (Lily)

Graduation day was not as gray for George Marshall as it might have been without Lily.

Years later General George C. Marshall often recalled his senior year at VMI as almost pleasant for several different reasons. For one thing, being First Captain of cadets put him in charge of the entire corps, and that was an important responsibility. He enjoyed his final year, too, because he played football and had a fine season, winning All Southern Conference honors as a left tackle. For another thing, he had managed to stay at the mid-section of his class in grades and would graduate. But he enjoyed that year, most of all, because of Lily.

Lily was a wonderful surprise in his VMI life. If he had not played football, and she had not played the piano, George Marshall might never have met Lily Coles.

While walking back to the barracks from football practice one evening, George stopped to listen to the beautiful piano music coming from a house nearby. He heard, as he later said, "some of the same airs my mother used to play, and of which I was very fond." After that day, he stopped often to listen, until finally one evening; Lily's mother invited him in, to meet the music maker.

George found the piano player as lovely to see, as her music was to hear. She played as well as any concert pianist, Marshall often said, and he never tired of listening to her. She lived with her mother on Letcher Avenue, barely outside the Limits Gate of VMI, and was a noted beauty in Lexington, with auburn hair, a beautiful complexion, and violet-blue eyes. Lily was popular and somewhat of a flirt, and had dated many cadets, including George's own brother, Stuart, who attended VMI six years ahead of George. Yet, George was the one who won her heart. Soon after they met, Lily told her mother, "I'm going to marry him."

When George C. Marshall met Elizabeth Carter Coles, he fell head over heels in love! What little free time he could manage away from his classes, football, and military routines, he spent with Lily. Although it was forbidden, and he knew it, George risked everything just to visit her. He often "ran the block" (sneaked out of Barracks after 'lights out'). If he had been caught, he could have been expelled, and that might have ruined his chances of being an army officer. But luck was with him, his roommates helped him, and he didn't get caught.   Later, he claimed that his only defense for breaking VMI rules was: "I was very much in love."

In June of 1901, the prospect of George C. Marshall becoming an officer was uncertain. The necessary army tests loomed darkly on his horizon. Life for George Marshall, beyond that rainy day of graduation, was a cloudy forecast with chances of scattered showers and possibly a storm or two!

Reporting for Duty

Chapter 2

In the Meantime

September 1901 - February 1902

In the meantime, since he could not take the army tests until September, George C. Marshall took a job. He was twenty years old and engaged to be married. Army regulations declared that he could not marry before he received a commission nor could he be commissioned before he turned twenty-one. His birthday was the last day of December, six months away! Taking a job was a good idea.

In the early 1900s, it was important that a man be able to support a wife because most women did not work outside the home. He needed to find another possible profession, just in case he did not receive a commission. Luckily, a solution presented itself.

Marshall's first paying job, and the only one he ever held in the private domain, was at the Danville Military Institute in Danville, Virginia. The head of the school, Colonel Isaac H. Saunders, an 1884 VMI graduate, always hired a new VMI graduate to be his school's commandant of cadets. In 1901, he hired George C. Marshall.

DMI was an all-male, private, prep school with about ninety boys of elementary and high school ages, divided into two companies and a small band. Marshall had a room in the barracks with the students and was given the complimentary title of major. He put on his new uniform and polished up the boots and brass. Outside, his booming voice shouted out the orders, while he conducted the boys' marching drills. He was getting paid to do what he enjoyed doing, but there was one catch. The job included teaching!

Major Marshall was assigned to teach subjects that he had never done well in, such as spelling and English, arithmetic and algebra.

Danville Military Institute, Danville, Virginia

But he also taught history, which he had learned to love as a boy., and instructed the cadets in battalion drills and proper military procedures, which he had learned at Virginia Military Institute, of course.

Once, many years after 1901, some DMI ex-cadets gathered for a reunion, and they remembered Major Marshall "for being a strict disciplinarian, especially in drilling." Willis Dance, who became a VMI cadet after attending DMI, said that Marshall was, "a fine looking young man dressed in his blue uniform." Holt Lyon, a 1901 cadet corporal, told of the day Major Marshall watched as he put his company through their military paces, and then dismissed them. The major had told him, "Sheep could have done better."

When General Marshall died in October of 1959, his obituary in *The New York Times* failed to mention the Danville school. Milton Herman, a DMI cadet of 1901, wrote a letter to the editors addressing their mistake. In his letter about Marshall, he wrote, "Never was any teacher so admired as he was by those under his instruction. He showed them the traits that marked his career throughout: reserve, keen attention to his duties, and strict adherence to principles."

In late September of 1901, George Marshall traveled to Governor's Island, New York to take the Army examinations. Forrest C. Pogue wrote that George Marshall went to New York a few days before the examination to visit his father's friend, John Wise. When Marshall was seeking permission to take the examinations, Mr. Wise had written a letter of introduction to President William McKinley for him. This time Mr. Wise wrote a letter to Major General John Brook saying, "This boy has the very highest testimonials ...General Shipp (VMI superintendent)...regards him as one of the fittest pieces of food for gunpowder turned out by his mill (VMI) for many years."

On September 23, the examinations began and went on for four days. His highest scores were in history and general math, and one of his lowest scores was in geography. The second two sections of the examination were concerned with his "morals and physique." The Army needed physically fit officers with clean records of behavior, and honorable character. Marshall was a strong Episcopalian and one of the few cadets who made it through VMI

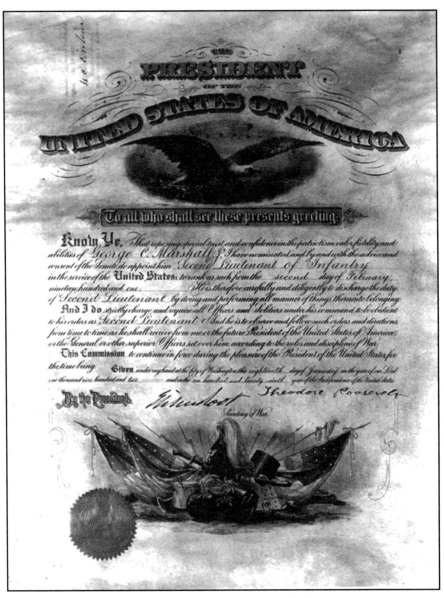

Marshall's U.S. Army commission

with no demerits on his record! He scored 100% in both morals and physique. He had an average score of 84.8 on the entire, three-part test, so he obviously didn't score 100% on the academic part!

On his application, George Marshall listed his three choices of the Army branches with Artillery first, Infantry second, and Cavalry third. After the tests were over, he went back to Danville, resumed his teaching and drilling of the DMI cadets, and waited for the test results. And he waited and waited, and waited some more.

By December 5, he could stand the suspense no longer. George asked his father to ask John Wise if he had heard anything. Mr. Wise asked the War Department what they knew about the results of George Marshall's test. Had he passed or had he not? Of course, George had passed, and with the highest score of all the applicants, the War Department officials had just failed to notify *him*!

On December 12, 1901, George C. Marshall wrote to General Shipp that "the news" was an early and "acceptable Christmas present." He resigned his position at Danville Military Institute and prepared to assume his new one in the Army. George spent Christmas in Lexington with his fiancée, Lily Coles, and her mother. They could finally make their wedding plans.

The orders naming him a second lieutenant were issued a few days after his birthday, on January 4, 1902. His appointment was confirmed on January 13, and Marshall's only regret was that he was assigned to the Infantry instead of the Artillery. Since he had requested the Artillery branch, he asked if he could change. He was refused. The Artillery was not taking newly commissioned officers from civilian status, only from West Point graduates. Maybe later, he was told, he could change with an Artillery officer who wanted to be an Infantry officer. That never happened.

George Catlett Marshall, Jr. took the oath before a notary public and was commissioned in Uniontown, Pennsylvania on February 3, 1902 and five days later his military orders arrived. He was ordered to report for duty on February 13, at Fort Myer, Virginia. He would be on his way to the Philippine Islands by the end of the month. At last, he was in the United States Army!

He had his commission and his orders, and ten days before reporting for duty. He also had a promise to keep.

Marshall-Coles wedding party - February 11, 1902
L-R: Marie Marshall, Lily Coles, George C. Marshall, Jr., Stuart Marshall, Laura Bradford Marshall
George C. Marshall, Sr., Mrs. Walter Coles

On February 9, Lieutenant George C. Marshall went from Uniontown to Lexington to be married. The next day his parents, his sister, Maria, his brother, Stuart, and his best friend, Andrew Thompson, arrived to join him there. The wedding took place in the house where George and Lily had first met.

A small group of friends and relatives gathered in the parlor, along with the minister. They mingled and talked and talked and mingled. After what she thought was enough socializing, it is reported that Lily turned to George and said, "Come on, George, let's get married." Edmund Coles, Lily's brother, 'gave his sister away' in the ceremony conducted by the Rev. R. J. McBryde of the Robert E. Lee Memorial Episcopal Church on the evening of February 11, 1902.

The next day the newlyweds rode the train to Washington, D.C. for a one-day honeymoon, staying at the New Willard, a most fashionable hotel. On February 13th, George walked along to the War Department in the State-War-Navy Building (now the Executive Office Building) at 17th and F streets on the west side of the White House and reported to the office of the Adjutant General with his orders. He also reported the news that he had just been married. Knowing they would be separated for about two years, the understanding officer allowed Marshall five more days before reporting for duty.

Even if wives had been permitted to go with junior officers, Lily could not have gone so far away from home. She had a heart condition that limited her physical activities and required her to live in a calm manner. Her quiet life style did not bother George, but leaving her behind did. George adored Lily, and always did whatever he could to make her happy. Still, he had to leave.

Northern Philippine Islands

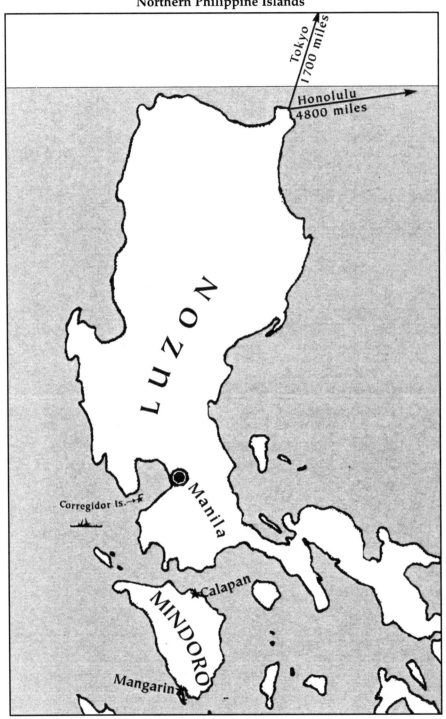

Map by Dr. Larry I. Bland,

Reporting for Duty

Chapter 3

Forward March, By George!

February 1902 – December 1903

Lily went home to Lexington to live with her mother, and George headed off to the Philippines. He had his orders, and was anxious to get to work as a soldier. He traveled from Fort Myer, Virginia to Fort Slocum, New York and on to California by train. From San Francisco, he left on the transport ship *Kilpatrick* on April 12, 1902, for Manila in the Philippine Islands. There, he met his assigned group, Company G of the 30th Infantry Regiment.

In 1902, the United States had control of the Philippine Islands because of the Spanish American War, which had ended four years earlier. War-like struggles between guerrillas and the American soldiers had lasted for several years, but by the time George C. Marshall arrived, the worst of the fighting was over, and he did not see combat. He met up with other enemies.

Marshall's main foes turned out to be disease, the weather, and boredom. Many of the 34,000 American soldiers stationed in the Philippines were not trained for the Army, but were criminal prisoners or vagrants gathered from the roughest and toughest segments of American life. Lieutenant Marshall was younger than many of the men he had to command. What a change from the world of VMI!

When George C. Marshall arrived in Manila, a cholera epidemic that had already killed thousands of people in the Philippines was still spreading. Cholera is a disease spread through unsafe water, dirty hands, unwashed utensils and raw or unclean food. It dehydrates the body and is usually fatal.

Cholera was a worry, but not his only one. His first army adventures began at sea. Because of the cholera epidemic no more ships would be going to Mindoro during the next three months, yet Marshall needed to get from Manila to his assigned village, Calapan, on the island of Mindoro. One last ship taking passengers to Mindoro was ready to leave Manila, just as Marshall was, and he obtained permission to board it.

Lieutenant Marshall settled himself on the ship and it sailed off, across Manila Bay. Then, it stopped. The ship was placed under a quarantine that kept it, and everyone on it, sitting at sea in the scorching, tropical heat for five days. The object of the quarantine was to protect new arrivals, like Marshall, from cholera by keeping them away from the island. Stuck out in the bay, sitting hour after hour on a boat with a metal deck, in the relentless heat was boring and uncomfortable. George Marshall wanted some action, and he also wanted to cool off. He found action, all right.

In telling Forrest C. Pogue Marshall recalled, "The boat was greasy and dirty . . . the heat was terrific . . . Finally, another young officer and myself . . . went down the rope ladder and dove off into the bay and started to swim . . . we had hardly gotten into the water when . . . Padre Isidro Sanz (a priest) . . . began screaming to us and pointing . . . We looked around and there were two sharks with their fins sticking up. We had a swimming race to that rope! I went right over the fellow's head going up that rope. I never showed such strength and agility in my life as going up the side of that boat. That was the only cooling experience that we had, and it could hardly be called that."

The vessel was finally released from the quarantine, allowed to sail again, and headed for a harbor when more trouble began. Escaping from a shark was one scary way to relieve boredom, but they ran straight into another kind of trouble and could not escape it as quickly.

General Marshall told the story like this: "We went by Corregidor, and were waved at, and jeered by the garrison, all of whom seemed to have bath towels. Then we turned down the coast . . .We were not aware at the time that we had disregarded the typhoon signals . . ." In a short time, they learned what the white towels meant. A typhoon is dangerous for a ship!

"I am not exaggerating at all when I state that the boat would tilt over until the lifeboats on the upper deck would go in the water

. . . and it would seem like it (the ship) was never going back again. Then it would go up and go to the other side . . ."

The ship's captain was so scared that he left his command post on the ship's bridge. The man at the wheel, the first mate, took a smash to his ribs, and he left, too. Then the engine room flooded, and the crew panicked. Lieutenant Marshall and another lieutenant, a man named Daly, took over the ship and forced the crew, at gunpoint, to stay in the engine room and run the ship. The vessel was powered by steam engines, and the engines required fires to heat water for making steam. The Filipino crewmen stayed in the engine room. Even if they didn't speak much English, they understood guns!

Then Marshall and Daley figured they could steer the ship into shore, since the captain and the first mate were unable to do it. "The two of us got the wheel and, of course, we turned it in the wrong direction and were heading right into these forbidding looking mountains . . . and we just battled that thing (the storm) all night long . . . It was a nerve-wracking experience . . . Finally, . . .we made Batangas Bay."

George C. Marshall had outsmarted a shark and a typhoon before he reached his post on Mindoro! His next battle was with cholera. The cholera arrived there slightly ahead of him. He and the other officers, along with the soldiers living in Calapan, were quarantined and confined to their barracks.

The officers had slightly better living quarters than the soldiers did, which wasn't saying much. Calapan was the island capital, surrounded by hills and jungle, and in a remote area about 8500 feet above sea level, with a population of about five thousand. The houses were mostly grass huts built on stilts. Being confined, the troops had nothing to do, and since the soldiers had nothing to do, neither did the officers.

General Marshall said, "I remember our principal amusement was to sit after meals with an old phonograph, the kind that you see on advertisements, 'His Master's Voice.' We had one recording device. So, we would shave our one wax record . . . and we would record our amateur performances . . . with only about eight of us . . . we would make a record, and then we would play it back and get great amusement out of that."

20

Company G, 30th Infantry at Santa Mesa Garrison near Manila, Philippine Islands, 1903. Lieutenant George C. Marshall, first row - 5th from left.

Marshall also remembered, "The epidemic made eating a very tiresome chore." They had to eat to keep up their strength against the disease, but the main source of food was canned. Nothing fresh or uncooked could be eaten. Water had to be boiled and reboiled before they could drink it.

He said, "Everything had to be boiled. The fingernails had to be cleaned; the hands had to be washed in hot water . . . mess kits had to be washed in two or three runs of hot water. You had to enforce these things very carefully or they [the troops] would skimp on them. A very little skimping would cost you your life."

The cholera epidemic took many Filipino lives on Mindoro, but no U.S. soldiers died. The quarantine, and the discipline of extreme cleanliness, that Marshall helped enforce, was effective. The soldiers' good health remained, but not their good tempers. They grew tired of confinement, of the boring routine of cleanliness, and especially tired of being together. They needed a break!

Just before July 4, the quarantine was lifted, and the officers in charge declared it time for a celebration. The commanding officer, Enoch R.L. Jones, decided they should have a field day and planned a range of events. Lieutenant Marshall was put in charge of carrying through on the C.O.'s plan. Everyone was under orders to attend the festivities whether they wanted to or not.

George C. Marshall was resourceful in planning a different kind of celebration. He went from officer to officer and collected money to offer as prizes in the athletic events. There was very little for which to spend money on in Calapan, so the officers were generous in their donations.

The soldiers were not told about the prize money. They were still grouchy from their recent confinement, the weather was muggy, and they were in no mood for athletics, competitions, or games of any kind. It was too hot to run, and who cared, anyway? When the hundred-yard dash was called, only three men showed up for the race.

Marshall later said, "They ran the hundred yard dash. I gave the number one man twenty dollars, the number two man fifteen dollars, and the number three man ten dollars. Well, as a soldier's pay was only $13.00 a month, those were huge prizes."

The soldiers perked right up, and when the second race was announced there were so many runners they couldn't all compete. Spirits rose quickly as the competition for prizes increased, although the prizes were less.

[Fifty years later, General Marshall went to a veteran's reunion in Winona Lake, Indiana of the 30th Infantry soldiers. The group gave him a tremendous welcome. The chairman of the organization, Clyde A. Benton, was the soldier who had won the twenty dollars in the first foot race of that July celebration.]

Then, with a friendly sergeant's help, Lieutenant Marshall organized a horse race with some of the wild ponies the army had captured on the island. Men rode bareback down the street of the town. The horse race was followed by a bicycle race. The men were finally relaxing, laughing, and having more fun than they had had in three months.

Later that day, Marshall discovered he was also supposed to organize a show for the evening entertainment. The sergeant who had helped with the horse races volunteered to arrange a stage, a curtain, and footlights for the show. During the performance that night, while some soldiers were performing, the sergeant came to Marshall again. He said, "This is going pretty well, Lieutenant, . . . (but) up in the guardhouse is the most popular man here and he clogs and sings, and if we could just get him here, it would help us a lot." Marshall said, "I'll go get him."

George C. Marshall went to the colonel and told him, "I want the man that's in the guardhouse that is a wonderful dancer and sings and is very popular . . . I want you to get the adjutant to tell the officer of the day to let me have him tonight." Together they talked to the adjutant.

After awhile, when the curtain (which was just a piece of water-proof canvas) was opened, Marshall remembered, " . . .and they found him dancing, with the band playing, they just cheered to the echo. He put on a grand performance. He was out of irons, he was out of the doghouse, and the whole garrison was cheering him. He made it quite a show . . . the men were crazy about it . . . he did encore after encore."

The sergeant talked to Marshall again, then Marshall talked to the Colonel, and it was decided that the man could be paroled to the garrison, which meant the men would be responsible for him, and keep him out of trouble. That made everybody happier, especially the man who had been in jail!

The show was a great success. The applause was wonderful, it "lasted for about two days" according to George Marshall, and the whole day's events gave the troops a boost in their spirits. Keeping up the spirits and the morale of troops always concerned him.

After Calapan, Marshall was transferred to another section of Company G in Mangarin, also on Mindoro. Mangarin was smaller than Calapan, in fact it was hardly more than a deserted village, but there was a convent which the soldiers were supposed to guard. There, he took on more responsibility because he was the highest-ranking officer on that end of the island. From July until mid-September, with the help of First Sergeant William Carter and Sergeant August Torstrup, Marshall ran the post, managed the Army routine, kept things running smoothly, and survived.

Resourceful George C. Marshall learned quickly, and he had a talent for depending on the skill and the experience of his subordinates. When he needed a job done, he found the best person for it, made the assignment, and left him alone to do it. Marshall's VMI training gave him a firm understanding of duty and the importance of doing one's best, whenever and wherever needed. Marshall developed experience and added to his knowledge of duty and of commanding men during his time in Mangarin. He even learned to deal with crocodiles!

"I remember one affair. We worked out from Mangarin, sailed around, and landed some distance out, and there was a little barrios (tiny village). We were going through that in order to get on firm land away from the swamps, in order to get up into the mountains. We found these people working on a pony . . . a crocodile had almost bitten off the hip of the pony. . . They were just sewing him up without any regard to the pony's feelings, and that horrified the men.

"Right close by this stream, rather narrow, but deep and heavy brush on either side. We went into this stream single file. I had seven men. They were behind me and holding their rifles up and their ammunition belts up to keep them clear from the water. When we got about two-thirds of the way across, there was a splash up above us (upstream) and some fellow yelled, 'crocodile.'

"In about a second they all plunged ahead. They ran over me. I was ground right down to the bottom. Their feet went up my back and over me and up the other side. I finally came to the surface pretty well done up."

Marshall was in a situation that took some fast thinking. The men had not intended to run over him or to hurt him, but in their panic, they did. He made a decision. "I got to the surface . . . went up the steep bank where the seven men were standing . . . looking very guilty and very unsure of themselves . . . I took my position in front of them, wet and covered with mud, and fell them in (called them to attention) very formally. I then gave them "right shoulder arms," faced them to the right and marched them down into the stream and clear to the other side.

"As they reached the other bank, I gave them 'to the rear, march.' They came back up out of the crocodile stream. Then I halted them, faced them toward me, inspected their guns, and . . .gave them 'fall out.' Then we started our excursion up into the mountains . . . They never referred to it. I never referred to it . . . I had done what I think was just about right."

George C. Marshall quickly decided and acted upon a course of action that restored his right of command, and the confidence of those he led. His imagination in commanding troops was rare for someone only twenty-one.

In January of 1903, his company moved to Santa Mesa, east of Manila, where he lived almost comfortably in a real house, instead of a native hut, with other officers. In Santa Mesa, he began horseback riding, the recreation that he preferred throughout his life above all others. In the early days of his riding, a horse fell on him, severely spraining his ankle. He spent several weeks on crutches and was excused from duty.

While he was laid up with the ankle problem, he volunteered to help the inspector of the headquarters examine the property accounts of the soldiers. Some of them were awaiting financial clearance before they would return to the United States. As George C. Marshall dug through piles and stacks of receipts and vouchers,

U.S. Patrol, Phiippine Islands, 1902

he learned a great deal about Army rules of accounting and expenses. That experience proved very useful to him later.

In September, Marshall moved to the last and most unpleasant of his Philippine assignments. His detachment was sent to Malahi Island, in Leguna de Bay, to guard Army prisoners. The living conditions were terrible and the work depressing. The prisoners were murderers, deserters, or as Marshall later recalled, "the dregs of the Army . . . the toughest crowd of men I have ever seen. You had to count them twice every night," because they might escape. Luckily, that assignment was soon over.

The 30th Infantry was ordered home, back to the States, and they set sail from Bataan on November 13, 1903 on the Army transport *Sherman*. When the ship stopped in Japan and Hawaii, George purchased trinkets and souvenirs for Lily. His next assignment was to be in the heartland of his home country, but first he was headed for the land of his heart — to Virginia where his lovely bride, Lily, was waiting.

Reporting for Duty

Chapter 4

Over Hill, Over Dale

December 1903 – July 1913

By December of 1903, Lieutenant Marshall was back in the States. His new assignment was at Fort Reno, in the Oklahoma Territory, west of Oklahoma City, an area almost as remote and primitive as the Philippines. At Fort Reno were four companies of the 24th Infantry, a troop of the 8th Cavalry and two companies of the 30th Infantry, with Marshall still in Company G. Lily did not go to Fort Reno right away with George, but she did join him there several months later.

George C. Marshall described Fort Reno to Forrest C. Pogue like this: "It was an old frontier post . . . The reservation was about sixteen miles square and was next to the Cheyenne and Arapahoe (Indian) Reservations right across the river from us.

Fort Reno, in 1904 was "old Army," which meant strict traditions of personal appearance and actions was the rule. A soldier, especially an officer, was expected to maintain an immaculate uniform with glistening metal work, and highly shined shoes. The men at Fort Reno were concerned with following orders, exact routines, and memorizing the Army rulebooks. Marshall read all the books and memorized all the necessary facts needed to be qualified for his duty there.

As often happened during his army career, George C. Marshall was taken from the regular, routine duty and given a special assignment. In the summer of 1905, George C. Marshall, along with ten other officers, was in his own words, "send down to Fort Clark in Texas to map about two thousand square miles . . . along the Rio Grand and Devil's River out from Del Rio towards Sanderson, Texas . . . (for the hardest service I ever had in the army."

28

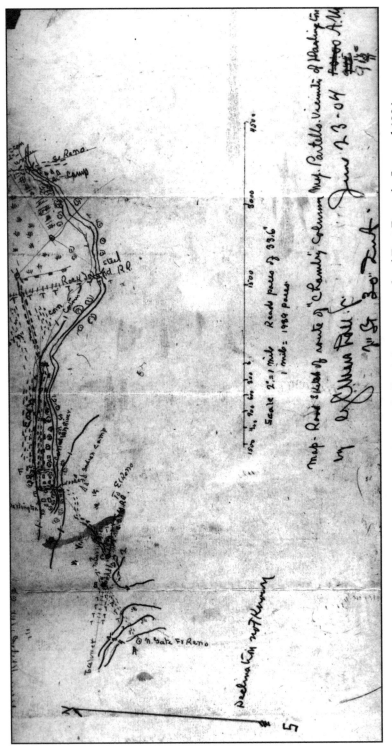

Part of a map drawn by George C. Marshall of the area north of Fort Reno in June of 1904

He was given two horses for himself, and an escort wagon and a four-line mule team driven by Nate Cox. He also had twenty pack mules with their packer, a fifty-eight year-old soldier named Davis, a sergeant to help with the sketching, and a cook, all from the 1st Cavalry. They had a difficult time finding enough food and water, for the country side was rugged. It was July and extremely hot. As he recalled, "The thermometer would go up to 130. I went in there weighing about 165 or 170 ad came out weighing 132 pounds . . . the old packer and myself were without water for eighteen hours and had to travel pretty nearly fifty miles . . . I had to walk the track and count the rails. That would give me an exact measurement which I needed as a sort of baseline. I got my distances otherwise from the odometer on the wheel of the wagon and from the time scale on the walking of my horse. This was an endurance contest of the first class."

After three months of living out in the Texas badlands, and with his surveying and mapping mission complete, Marshall and his crew returned to the base camp at Fort Clark. When the captain at Fort Clark, Malin Craig, first saw Marshall, he didn't think that man could be an officer. Lieutenant Marshall was sun tanned almost black and wearing a old Panama hat which a mule had bitten the top out of, so Craig wouldn't look at Marshall but talked to the sergeant who was with him, instead. [Thirty-four years later, Marshall succeeded Malin Craig as Chief of Staff of the U.S. Army.]

Marshall did not like this assignment, but he did it. And he did the best job he could do of mapping "his part of Texas." Marshall's map-making efforts paid off. The chief engineer officer of the Southwestern Division told George C. Marshall that his map was, "the best one received, and the only complete one." After so much hard work, the commanding general at San Antonio, granted Marshall four months leave, which he gladly accepted.

In the fall of 1905, he went back to Lexington for a visit with Lily, and on to Pennsylvania to visit his parents for the first time in three years. In Uniontown, he found that places and people had changed while he was away. The brick house where George was born was gone, the yard had been leveled and covered with fill dirt, and in place of the house stood The West End Theater. His parents had moved into an apartment because his mother needed less house to care for, and his father looked older, moved slower, and was no longer the busy man about town he once was. His sister and brother were both soon to be married. Yes, things had certainly changed.

Still, George went about searching for places and people that were familiar. One of his childhood friends had died, and George went to visit the boy's mother. In the yard at her house, George found Trip, his friend's old dog, a shorthaired terrier, lying "on the stones by the old pump in the sun, . . .his black coat . . . turned almost brown.

"He paid no attention to me—he didn't bark at me—he was so old he was just indifferent . . . That was quite a blow because Trip was one of the close companions of my youth. So I sat down . . . and succeeded in petting him, although he rather resented it . . . I talked to him quite a long time, trying to renew my youth, and was very much distressed that he didn't remember me at all.

"After, I suppose five or ten minutes, he took a careful sniff of me, then he sniffed at me two or three times, and then he just went crazy. He had finally gotten a scent in his old nostrils and he remembered me. That was the most flattering thing that occurred to me on that short visit home after so many years of not being there."

When Marshall returned to Fort Reno, Lily went along. If an officer had a wife along, his living conditions on the post became smewhat improved. He was assigned a house instead of a tent. Even in her delicate health condition, Lily enjoyed being an Army wife, part of the time. Marshall said, "An army wife in those days had to face a great deal. If she could get a hold of a servant, she was in luck. But (an officer's) pay was very slender."

One of George C. Marshall problems in 1906 was his budget. The starting pay for a second lieutenant was $116.67 per month. Out of it he had to pay for his uniforms, food, and the required arms and equipment, from saber and revolver to his field glasses, bed roll, and mess kit. He said, ". . . my pay was so limited, I had to watch every cent. I had to keep track of it down to the last dime. My struggle was to come out ahead. I really wasn't much interested in whether it was $1.50 or $10.50 ahead for the month, but it was to be ahead and not getting behind."

At that time in his career, he was moving often and whenever he moved, he paid the expenses. "I always struggled in those days to have a month's pay ahead . . . a sum on hand that would be equivalent of the cost of moving . . . the government didn't move our wives and families . . . We got a very limited allowance for packing our things up . . . we got literally nothing."

Marshall enjoyed hunting and fishing in the area of Fort Reno, and he recalled to Forrest C. Pogue that, "The hunting was superb. We went shooting almost every day of the year for something or other . . . At the time I was a pretty good shot . . . I would shoot ducks that would fall on the tents . . . I remember on one occasion Mrs. Marshall and I were early for breakfast, and we heard the quail calling in a little sumac grove near us, and I went out there. In about thirty minutes, I came back for breakfast and I had twelve quail. Actually, I think I had fifteen, but I don't want to claim that (many)."

In 1906, George was offered a chance to attend the Infantry and Cavalry School at Fort Leavenworth, and he accepted. He was just in time! Shortly after he was admitted, the Army rules changed. From then on, an officer had to be a captain or a major in order to enter the school. He was only a second lieutenant, so if he had not entered when he did, he probably would not have entered at all. Had he not gone to Leavenworth, he would have missed out on several years of important military training. That change in direction greatly effected his career.

George C. Marshall realized he would have a rough path to follow in the first year of his new schooling. There were fifty-three other officers in the class who were all older, more experienced, and better students than he was. One day George overheard two classmates discussing the names of those most likely to succeed and be kept on for the second year. His name was not one of those mentioned. That was all it took for George C. Marshall to decide that he would be among the ones to stay.

He remembered that in 1897 his brother had thought he would disgrace the Marshall family name at VMI with his poor grades. George had proved Stuart wrong, and had not failed. He would not fail this time, either. He set to work, and left nothing to chance.

Infantry and Cavalry School, Fort Leavensworth, Kansas, 1907.
Second Lieutenant Marshall - fourth row, second from left.

"I finally got into the habit of study, which I never really had before. I revived what little I had carried with me out of college and I became pretty automatic at the business . . . it was the hardest work I ever did in my life."

Much of his work and study was memorizing facts and formulas. Then he was supposed to apply what he had memorized in his classroom recitations or on written tests. There was fierce competition among the officers for grades, and their marks were ranked to the .01 percent. Differences could be small, but vital.

One day Marshall scored 100 on a map exercise and his friend scored 95.17, yet his friend ranked 47th among the fifty-four students. The intense focus on grades may not have meant that real learning was taking place for anybody, but Marshall knew that high grades were important to his career.

He had the ability to apply his attention to his studies without distraction, and, he used his wife's frail health as a reason for not going out at night or socializing often. Their quiet lifestyle fit his needs well, and he liked staying home to study. Sometimes, though, his mind just wouldn't quit thinking and George C. Marshall found sleeping difficult. He said, "I would get up and shine my boots . . . I had very shiny boots."

His hard work and study paid off for him. At the end of the first year, after all the grades and rankings were averaged, George C. Marshall was first in the class. He was number one, just as he had intended to be. He was, of course, scheduled to continue for the second year. The second year at Fort Leavenworth (1907-1908) was much easier for Marshall, less of a grind, and more fun. He did not worry about class ranking, but that did not keep him from working hard.

"My reading . . . was helpful, as was my study of past operations. My habits of thought were being trained. While . . . I learned little I could use . . . I learned how to learn. I began to develop along more stable lines."

Following the two years of study at Fort Leavenworth, George C. Marshall was appointed to stay on for two more years as an instructor in the Army Service Schools and Staff College. He taught engineering and military art. He was promoted to First Lieutenant in March of 1907, and still all the men he instructed were higher in rank than he was.

For about three weeks in July of 1909, Marshall was assigned to duty with the Pennsylvania National Guard, fairly close to his hometown. He took some time off to visit his parents, and afterwards, was always glad he did. It was the last time he saw his father. When his National Guard duties were finished, he hurried off toward Virginia.

Along the way, he was to spend the night with a classmate friend from Fort Leavenworth, First Lieutenant Benjamin D. Foulois at Fort Myer, Virginia. Foulois was considered by some Leavenworth students to be somewhat odd. He frequently talked about the Wright Brothers and their new flying machine. He thought it might have an impact on military tactics someday.

When Marshall arrived at Fort Myer, he was surprised to find that his friend had, on that 30th day of July, been the navigator-passenger on the flying machine with Orville Wright, going at least forty miles per hour, for twenty miles. Lieutenant Foulois' apartment was full of reporters, all wanting to hear about the historic flight! Perhaps George Marshall thought maybe that airplane idea would amount to something, after all!

George went with Lily to visit her relatives in the "Green Mountain section" of Albemarle County, in " . . . that isolated part . . . beyond Carter's Bridge fifteen miles south of Charlottesville." He spent many days riding horseback along the tree-shaded lanes and taking canoe rides on the James River. However, his temperament did not allow him to relax all of the time. He so enjoyed the Virginia summertime countryside that he wanted to do something helpful for the county, and he did.

In *Education of a General*, Forrest C. Pogue wrote that Marshall borrowed a buggy, tied a handkerchief on one wheel, measured the circumference of the wheel, and, with the help of some neighbors, set out to map the southern part of the county. Day after day he pursued his project of measuring the distances "between plantations and crossroads, between infrequent hamlets and innumerable fords, by counting the revolutions of this wheel." Then, from his computations, he drew a map.

In September of 1909, George C. Marshall's father died of a stroke in Uniontown. When his father died, George C. Marshall knew a connection to his past was broken, he had finally left his

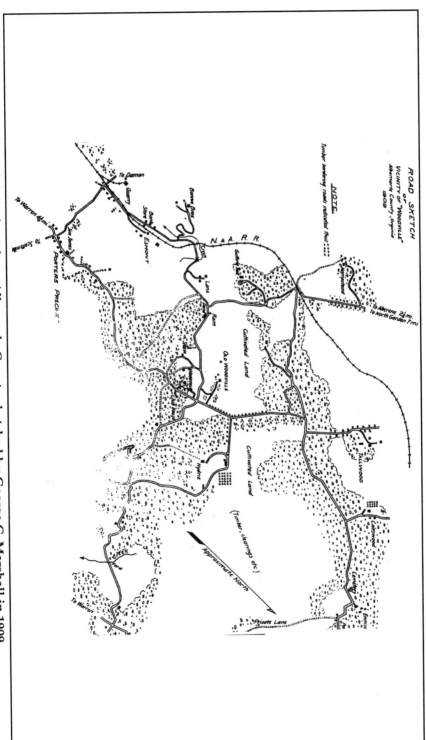

A map of part of southern Albemarle County sketched by George C. Marshall in 1909.

boyhood home, completely. His father left no will, so the three children assigned their shares of his twenty-six thousand dollar estate to their mother and thus provided her income for the remaining nineteen years of her life. Both of Marshall's parents are buried in Allegheny Cemetery in Pittsburgh.

During the summers, between sessions at Fort Leavenworth, Marshall worked with the National Guard at training camps in various states. The first summer he had only one week of duty, but the following summers he had longer assignments. Before going on leave, in 1910, he spent summer camp time in Karner, New York and in Massachusetts with the militia in Hingham and South Framingham, plus a week at the National Rifle Matches in Camp Perry, Ohio.

George and Lily returned to Fort Leavenworth for the 1909-10 school year. He had completed the schooling at Ft. Leavenworth, and two years of teaching. He began to wonder if he had made the right career choice. He wondered what his next assignment would be. Where would he be sent next? In order to stall that next move, he put in for the four months of leave that was due him, plus a fifth month at half pay, beginning in late August of 1910.

After the summer Guard duty was over in September, George and Lily Marshall finally took a honeymoon trip abroad to Europe. They toured England for more than a month and went on to France for a few weeks, five weeks in Italy and also in Austria. In Versailles, near Paris, they had an illegal picnic on the palace grounds but got away with it, because they asked the policeman to share their picnic with them. George and Lily had a lovely trip, all leisure and no work. Traveling for pleasure was good for renewing Marshall's spirit.

Traveling for work was different, but work was a necessity for a serious young officer trying to become a general. During the next three years, Marshall was sent to army posts in Arkansas, Texas, Massachusetts, New York, Minnesota, and in the summers of 1911-1913, Marshall worked in the summer camps of the New England area. He planned and directed large and complicated maneuvers that were new and exciting. The movements crossed state lines and involved multi-state forces of both National Guard and Regular Army troops.

Through his National Guard experiences, George C. Marshall gained skills as a teacher of military tactics. He learned how important well-planned maneuvers can be as a means of effective training. Later, he used his experiences in officer training, in preparing troops for military operations in World War I and II. Having good commanding officers that knew how to move massive forces of men and materials across combat zones covering hundreds of square miles was essential for a general.

George C. Marshall was an excellent teacher. One of his students, M.W. Clement, a lieutenant with the 13th Regiment of the 3rd Brigade of the Pennsylvania National Guard, who became president of the Pennsylvania Railroad, said of Marshall, "He had the ability to make everybody understand. A new world in military affairs opened itself up to the minds of the militia men."

While stationed in Texas City, near San Antonio, with the Fourth Infantry, Marshall was given an assignment to Company D of the Signal Corps as an assistant to Major George O. Squier, the chief signal officer. Here he tried setting up a practice communications center from which a commanding officer could direct troops without having to be with them. He selected three pilots to act as generals commanding two infantry outfits and one cavalry brigade. (One of the pilots was his friend, Lieutenant Benjamin Foulois, who flew with Orville Wright in 1909.) They reported to Marshall, who acted as chief of staff for the practice, by telephone and radio. Radio was the "high technology" of the time, somewhat like aeroplanes (airplanes).

One portable wireless (radio) transmitter, that required two men to crank it, was sent out with the cavalry unit. Marshall stayed at headquarters and directed the men in the field or the airplanes, having them report their location and what they saw by telephone or radio. Forrest C. Pogue wrote, "The historic first message that came back to headquarters was from the cavalry commander, who reported, 'I am just west of the manure pile.' What manure pile he was west of no one at headquarters ever found out." this may have been the beginning of walkie-talkies, radio, or telephone in army maneuvers!

Between the field telephones and the airplanes for observation, Major Squire found Lieutenant Marshall's plan impressive. He said that it appeared the airplane would become a military necessity in the future, and that Marshall had demonstrated the possibility of generals commanding troops from a safe distance without having to be in the actual battle.

From Texas, he was sent to Massachusetts, by way of two short National Guard assignments, one in Virginia, one in Pennsylvania. After serving short periods at many different army posts, moving often, and never settled anywhere for long, he was assigned to his second tour of duty in the Philippine Islands. Unlike his first trip to George was not leaving Lily at home this time.

Lieutenant George C. Marshall -- 1908 - Fort Leavenworth, Kansas

Over Hill, Over Dale

During the world wars, many children sang patriotic songs, such as the Army song, the Air Corps song, and the Navy and Marine hymns in school every day.This song, written by Edward L. Gruber in 1908 while he was stationed in the Philippine Islands, is played by bands at Army functions, parades, or ceremonies. You may have heard it; all Army veterans and soldiers stand when they hear it. Copied from the book "Sound Off!", these original words" were used until the early 1960s when new ones were issued.

A cassion is a wagon, pulled by horses, loaded with infantry provisions, equipment, ammunition, and such. In places where there were no roads, the going could be very tough. Here are the words to the official army song.

The Cassion Song or The Cassions Go Rolling Along

Over hill, over dale,
We have hit the dusty trail,
And the Caissons go rolling along.
In and out, hear them shout,
"Counter march and right about",
And those cassions go rolling along.

Chorus:
Then it's hi! hi! hee!
In the field artillery,
Shout out your numbers loud and strong,
For where e'er you go,
You will always know
That the Caissons go rolling along.

An Infantry adaptation of the song came along in 1918 and goes like this:

Over Hill, Over Dale

Over hill, Over dale, as we hit the dusty trail,
It's the doughboys that still carry on.
Smeared with mud, spitting blood,
That's the branch that takes the rub;
It's the doughboys that still carry on.

Chorus:
Then it's hi! hi! hee! The good old infantree!
Way out in front and going strong.
When we cross the Rhine, we will leave the guns behind,
But those doughboys will still carry on.
(Shout) Follow me

Reporting for Duty

Chapter 5

Same Song, Second Verse

July 1913 — July 1916

Lily was tired of moving from base to base, and was actually glad when George received new orders in 1913 for his second assignment to the Philippine Islands. They sailed from San Francisco on July 5, 1913 aboard the Army transport, *Logan*. The trip took about a month of sailing, with a stop in Hawaii and Guam. He reported to Fort McKinley and was assigned to Company F of the 13th Infantry.

Fort McKinley was a large and well-manned base with a full regiment of infantry (the 13th), a regiment of cavalry, a field artillery battalion, and attached signal and engineer units, all maintained at combat strength. This made it easier for the Army to carry out realistic war games than it would have been in the States. The commanding officer of the Philippine Department was General J. Franklin Bell, a general who was watching George C. Marshall's career with keen interest and had been impressed with his performance at Fort Leavenworth.

Lieutenant Marshall's immediate commanding officer was Captain E. J. Williams. Captain Williams had been a student at Fort Leavenworth, and Marshall had been his instructor. Things were a bit different when George C. Marshall had to take orders from his ex-student!

All in all, it was not a bad assignment to be in the Philippines. Marshall told Forrest C. Pogue, "The living conditions, of course, were very much better because you had very good houses and you had very good servants, . . .good general commissary to bring things out, so that you got good things to eat and sufficient fresh things. . . it was a tremendous improvement over the Philippines of the old days."

Philippine Islands, a Manila main street, 1913

Pogue writes "At Fort McKinley, where four to five thousand officers and men were billeted (lived in) buildings only completed in 1904, life was very much like peacetime army life in the States if one ignored the occasional green lizard that dropped into the soup, ants sometimes on parade over the living-room floor, the tarantula on the bridge table, plagues of grasshoppers, and, of course, the heat."

The natives ate the grasshoppers! They were served fried, or cooked and mashed into a paste-like spread. Marshall claimed that large grasshoppers with their legs still on were quite good to eat, and were cleaner meat to eat than pig or chickens. He told this story later: " Mrs. Marshall was having a card party, and I had to mash up these grasshoppers and spread them on crackers. We toasted the crackers a little bit, spread the mashed grasshoppers . . . and served it. When I came home, she told me that Lin, the cook, had done a very clever thing. He'd developed this new paste, and all the women were crazy about it and wanted to know what it was. Lin wouldn't tell them.

"When she found out they'd been eating mashed grasshoppers, I was excommunicated (expelled) around the neighborhood then for about three or four months . . . (I thought) I gave the ladies quite a treat."

Marshall had barely arrived in the Philippines when General Bell put him to work planning a practice invasion of Luzon to test the army's defense system against attacks from the sea. The 'White Force' (the attackers) had to attack the 'Brown Force' (the defenders) at Manila, and Marshall was made the adjutant of the 'White Force'. The troops had to be gathered from different sections of the Philippine Islands, brought together by boat and assembled at just the right time, in just the right place, and in just the right way.

On the way to the mock attack, the 'White Force's' chief of staff was taken ill, and went back to Manila. George C. Marshall replaced him and was put in command of nearly 5000 men. This was extremely unusual, since Marshall was only a lieutenant and many of the other officers outranked him. It was a stressful situation and a very difficult undertaking for Marshall, but he performed brilliantly.

Another young officer, Lieutenant Henry H. (Hap) Arnold, saw George C. Marshall lying on his back in a bamboo clump, glancing at a map and giving precise field orders for the advance on Luzon. Arnold wrote home to his wife that he had just seen a future chief of staff of the Army in action.

Marshall's company commander, Captain E. J. Williams, said, "This officer, for his years of service, age and rank, is one of the most completely equipped for military service it has been my lot to observe." He finished his lengthy praise of the lieutenant by adding that if Marshall is promoted to a rank higher than his own, ". . . I would be glad to serve under him." Marshall's work in the Philippines was so impressive that General Hunter Liggett later made Marshall his aide-de-camp (assistant).

However excellent Marshall's work was, his body objected to the strain and stress. Together with the tropical heat, the situation brought on his second attack of "neurasthenia," a common term at that time used to describe a medical condition meaning somewhere "between physical exhaustion and a nervous breakdown." Marshall described it as a "a tight dry feeling" and being unable to relax.

The doctors prescribed two weeks of rest in the hospital at Manila, and that was followed by an extended vacation with Lily in Japan. During the Philippine hot season, Lily usually went to Japan for several months at a time. She was in Japan when he became ill, so Marshall joined her there in 1914 for a two-month medical leave plus another two-month regular leave. He used that time for gaining back his health, and learning about the art of relaxation, which he never quite mastered.

He did learn to slow down somewhat, and not push himself so hard. While in Japan, Marshall took up horseback riding again, this time as a regular hobby, and rode thirty or forty miles a day. He also did a lot of walking as a form of regular exercise. Marshall said he found, "the weather was perfect, the scenery in some places magnificent," and all in all the vacation in Japan was a lift for his spirits and his health.

George and Lily, both in better physical health, returned to the Philippines from Japan on June 5, 1914. Marshall began riding his horse an hour or so before breakfast, a habit that he would keep for many years. He also took up tennis playing in the afternoon, and he bought a Model T Ford. The car helped him to keep Lily entertained and he wrote to a friend, "We ride from twenty to sixty miles almost every evening . . . The roads out here are wonderfully fine — so much better than the roads in the States . . ." and they enjoyed the scenery as well as the weather.

George C. Marshall was not one for taking things for granted, but frequently investigated their meaning by taking things apart. He didn't simply drive the Model T, he had to learn how it worked, so he took the engine apart and then discovered, "I was not at all mechanical, but I just had to do it." Luckily, one of his fellow officers was more of a mechanic than Marshall and helped him put it back together.

Another trait of George C. Marshall's was ambition. He liked to succeed at whatever he was doing, and when he felt he wasn't succeeding, he changed course and went in another direction. In February 1915, he was transferred to Company M of the 13th Infantry, and appointed aide-de-camp to General Hunter Liggett.

In October of 1915, he was discouraged with the progress of his career. He had been in the army for thirteen years and was still a lieutenant. He did not feel he was advancing as an officer. He began to consider getting out of the army and wrote to General E.W. Nichols, the superintendent at the Virginia Military Institute, asking for advice, telling Nichols:

"The absolute stagnation in promotion in the infantry has caused me to make tentative plans for resigning . . . the prospects for advancement in the Army are so restricted by law and by the accumulation of large numbers of men of nearly the same age all in a single grade (officer level) that I do not feel it right to waste all my best years in the vain struggle against insurmountable difficulties."

Nichols replied, "I would think twice and think long before I gave up my commission were I in your place . . . I would advise you to stick to it. If you do, I am sure in time you will be among the high ranking officers in the service."

Marshall must have listened to that advice. Both men knew that George C. Marshall was not a quitter, and probably felt he would stay in the Army, but neither man gave much thought to the war that was developing in Europe. If they did, they did not think the United States would become involved. Sadly, they would be thinking of little else a few months later.

Captain George C. Marshall talks with Major General J. Franklin Bell
Governor's Island, New York, 1917.

Reporting for Duty

Chapter 6

Over Here

July 1916 — June 1917

Lieutenant and Mrs. Marshall were in San Francisco, safely back in the States from the Philippines, by late June of 1916. He thought he was going to work for General John J. Pershing, but instead was assigned as an aide to Major General J. Franklin Bell and stationed at the Presidio in San Francisco, California.

Soon after his return, Marshall was called to Fort McDowell to appear before the committee in charge of promotions. After fourteen and a half years, Lieutenant Marshall became a captain in the U.S.Army. His promotion was done in short order, and without questions, but it did not become official until October.

In June, Congress had passed The National Defense Act, increasing the size of the U.S. Army and the National Guard. Federal supervision of the National Guard increased, and so did co-operation between the National Guard and the Army regarding new citizen-training programs. Experienced instructors, like George C. Marshall, were needed to prepare the men in the ways of defense, should they be called into active service. For the rest of the summer and into the next year, Marshall traveled from California to Utah, inspecting the camps that General Bell supervised and sometimes helping with the training.

Before Marshall's promotion to captain became official, General Bell needed him in California to assist in giving six weeks of summertime military training to newly enlisted men in the several camps designed for inexperienced, young, college-age men as well as older, business and professional men.

Marshall's first stop was in Monterey, California. A camp had been set up on the grounds of the plush Del Monte Hotel. General William L. Sibert was in charge, and all of the assisting officers were retired army officers. George C. Marshall, still a lieutenant, was supposed to report to General Bell what was wrong and what needed correcting.

Upon arrival, Marshall saw the beautiful and romantic setting. The luxury and wealth of the hotel mixed with the joy and sunshine, the peaceful ocean-side beauty of Santa Cruz, Pacific Grove, and Carmel were all areas contrasting sharply with the needs of a military camp. The young men, as well as the older ones, the lawyers, doctors, ministers, merchants, and bankers, were spending their own money to come to this 'camp' where they could mix the patriotic stimulus of military drill in the daytime, with the glamour and excitement of the Del Monte Hotel at night. Some had brought their wives because it was such " a beautiful and ideal spot" for a vacation. But for an army training camp?

Marshall later said, "I saw more Rolls Royce's and other fine cars around there than I had ever seen . . . before, and they all went to the Del Monte at night. General Bell had been so careful to caution these men [instructors] not to be too severe . . . on these fellows . . . and they were dealing with a very lively sporty lot . . . I mean sporty in the way of polo and football . . . their Rolls Royce cars . . . their wives or their sweeties . . . so that it was quite a set up."

George C. Marshall was there to identify the problems, to put things in order, and that was exactly what he meant to do. He set up his tent beside the path the men walked along when coming from their camp to supper at the hotel or for the evening's activities. His bedroll had not been unpacked since arriving from the Philippines, and he felt sure that the men in training had not yet seen a proper bed roll undoing. So there, beside the path, Marshall made a first-rate demonstration of how an officer should properly undo his bedroll.

General Marshall said, "They were all fascinated by seeing me open my bedding roll. All of the officers were already in camp when they (the new recruits) got down there, so they hadn't seen that. Well, here was an officer undoing his bedding roll, which was pretty fat and big around. I suppose there were fifteen or twenty lined up watching me, making a few clever remarks . . . .to which I paid no attention . . . the first thing on top, of course, was my saddle. But the next thing, under the saddle, were two of Mrs. Marshall's nightgowns . . . packed in at the last minute, and then a whole string of stuff of hers which didn't look anything like a bedding roll arrangement for the field. . . we had put everything that was left in the house in the bedding roll . . . before we went to the boat. That made me famous almost in a minute."

The men really enjoyed the incident, and they proudly escorted George C. Marshall to the hotel for dinner. There were speeches that night ". . . as to my field equipment. . . I came to know them very quickly that same night. They were awfully nice fellows."

The next day he made his rounds, looked over the camp, and watched the routines. Then he made his rounds again, and wrote a list of the faults he found. He showed the list to General Sibert and told the general what he had been ordered to do. George C. Marshall, a lieutenant, was criticizing a general and felt he should go carefully.

General Sibert said, "Yes, I was sent a copy of the orders." Marshall said, "I've prepared this as far as I've gotten today, and I think I should show it to you before I send it to him (Gen.Bell), because I am in a very embarrassing position."

However, General Sibert promptly issued orders to start the corrections. The next day Marshall made another round of the camp, listing more faults that needed to be corrected. He took those to General Sibert and again Sibert issued correction orders. General Sibert's adjutant was not happy with having a lower level officer correcting their methods of operation, but he sent the findings and the changes to General Bell, anyway.

He also sent a request to have Marshall detailed to the camp! The next morning George C. Marshall found himself in charge of a company of two hundred men! "But what made it worse was that I was put in charge of a different company every day. Well, that made it a very strenuous thing, because I couldn't really get control of them before I was taken on to the next company."

Once the needed changes were made in Monterey, Marshall was assigned to Fort Douglas, Utah for the same reason — to organize their camp. The job at Fort Douglas lasted a month, and was successful. When he left Fort Douglas, Lieutenant Colonel Johnson Hagood, Marshall's superior and the commander at Fort Douglas, said in his efficiency report on Marshall's work, "This officer is well qualified to command a division, with the rank of major general, in time of war, and I would like very much to serve under his command." In September, Marshall was back in San Francisco as General Bell's aide-de-camp.

America entered the (First) World War against Germany in April of 1917, and was sending soldiers to fight. General Bell was appointed the commander of the Army's Department of the East and ordered to Governor's Island, New York. George C. Marshall, as his aide, was sent ahead of the General to New York, arriving there on May 1, along with Lily and her mother.

As General Bell traveled by train from California, he became ill with the flu. He stopped for a visit with relatives in Kentucky, and after he arrived on Governor's Island, he secretly went to a nearby hospital for treatment. Because he was unable to work, his organizational duties fell to George C. Marshall. Marshall did everything Bell would have done, from answering the mail and phone calls to assigning duties.

All of Bell's staff was older and higher in rank than George C. Marshall, so everybody wanted to know where General Bell was, and why a lowly captain was giving the orders. Marshall said, "So he went off and left me with a staff of about fifteen old colonels at the head of all the various departments, and . . . all the pressure of the war was coming on."

The war did come on, and George C. Marshall 's skills were fully tested that month. He directed the setting up and organizing of twenty training camps for new and prospective officers. The new officers were being prepared for war in Europe. With twenty-five hundred (2500) men at each camp, there were major decisions and problems connected with outfitting and preparing the camps to feed and shelter nearly forty thousand men.

George C. Marshall demonstrated his organizing skills so well that General John J. Pershing asked for Marshall to be assigned to him, but then realized that Marshall was with Bell, so he dropped the request. Pershing left for Europe on May 28, 1917 as commander of the American Expeditionary Forces. Marshall wished he could have gone with him.

He got his wish in early in June when General William L. Sibert, as commander of the First Division, was also being sent to France. General Sibert remembered Marshall from the camp at Monterey, and he asked for George C. Marshall to be assigned to him, as his Operations Officer, much to Marshall' s delight. General Bell understood how much Marshall wanted the assignment, and that the assignment could mean a great deal to Marshall's career.

Because General Bell was not going to France, he agreed to the change. According to Marshall's account to Forrest C. Pogue, General Sibert "made my desk , my services, the headquarters for troops just coming in to go to Europe in the first convoy, which was to be the First Division." The new lieutenants reported to Captain Marshall, and as he recalled, "these were splendid looking young men . . . I remember the first ten that came in. Every one of them had gotten married the minute they got the note (their orders)."

Marshall remembered how scary and lonely it felt to be a newly married lieutenant going off to a foreign place. And these men were going to war. He allowed the men an extra few days before reporting for duty because the First Division was not quite ready to sail. During the war, he kept up with eight of the ten men, and all eight men died in France.

George C. Marshall, too, would soon be 'Over There'!

Over There

Over there, over there,
Send the word, send the word over there,
That the Yanks are coming, the Yanks are coming!
The drums rum-tumming everywhere.
So prepare, say a prayer,
Send the word, send the word to beware,
We'll be over, we're coming over,
And we won't be back till it's over, over there.

Copyright, Leo Feist, Inc.   Lyrics by George M. Cohan

Over There was a popular war song of the time. It was sung in France as well as in America, and by civilians as well as by the troops of doughboys on their way to war.

Reporting for Duty

Chapter 7

Over There

June 1917 – September 1919

"Finally, we started out and I felt the ship moving. So I thought I would get up and see this affair. It was certainly historic, our troops going to Europe. I got out on deck and it was about four in the morning or thereabouts. Anyway, it was just dimly light," George C. Marshall wrote in *Memoirs of My Services in the World War 1917-1918*.

Captain George C. Marshall was concerned about the lack of training the Army had provided its officers and enlisted men before putting them on a ship destined for war in France. The First Division simply was not ready for front-line combat. While worrying, and standing under the bridge on the ship, *Tenadores*, he saw the three-inch guns on a pedestal mount, and he thought: "Well, thank goodness. There is one thing that is organized, the Navy."

Then he learned that although the three-inch guns were mounted on the ship, there was no ammunition for them! He suddenly knew neither the Navy or the Army was organized and, as he wrote, "I thought, my God, even the naval part isn't organized and we're starting off to Europe!"

On June 26, 1917, the First Infantry Division of the American Expeditionary Forces (AEF) landed in France. George C. Marshall was the second man to go ashore, following closely behind his commander, General William Sibert.

A camping area had been set up on the outskirts of the town. General Sibert and his staff were taken out to see it. Marshall rode with a French officer, and tried out his skill of speaking French, which he had decided he wanted to do as much as possible.

". . . Intending to comment on the wonderful morning, I remarked, "Je suis tres beau aujourd'hui." He gave me an odd look and I mentally translated my remark." (Instead of saying, "It is a very beautiful day," Marshall had said, "I am very beautiful today," to the Frenchman.) "During the ensuing (next) twenty-six months I never spoke French again except when forced to."

George C. Marshall's French was, for sure, not as sharp as his organizational skills. The First Division was stationed near Neufchatel, at Gondrecourt, with the soldiers housed in half a dozen surrounding villages. As more and more troops arrived from the States, he was kept extremely busy with helping to settle and organize them.

Numerous details, plans, and specific orders were necessary for feeding, equipping and in billeting (housing) several thousand men. Outside kitchens, mess tents, sleeping tents, latrines, and medical facilities had to be built. Marshall wrote, "I became very much involved with all these things at the start . . . in locating the first four divisions . . . and seeing what they needed. . . I had to figure out what was required in the way of mess halls and bunkhouses and headquarters and hospital buildings and everything of that sort. Nobody advised me. They didn't have time. They just told me to do it."

Reinforcements were necessary. Three other divisions came in as fast as they could be transported from the States. The 2nd Division had Marine units, the 26th had the New England National Guard units, and the 42nd was the Rainbow Division with National Guard units from twenty-seven different states. Once the troops had places to sleep and eat, the training began.

The British, French, Italians and Russians (the Allies) had been fighting Germany and Austria-Hungary (the Central Powers) for three years before the Americans entered the war. The French and British high commands wanted to take the American troops and mix them in with their own, without waiting for the American officers to get any training done. Their forces had suffered severe troop losses and needed more men for combat, to replace their dead and wounded.

General John Pershing, Commander of the AEF (American Expeditionary Forces), became impatient with the long training time that officers like George C. Marshall felt the troops needed. He made the rounds of the division headquarters, often on short notice, looking for battle-ready units. One day in September of 1917 he came to review the First Division, with very short notice, and was not pleased with what he saw.

He came back again in early October, and watched a second demonstration of combat attack arranged by George C. Marshall and led by Major Theodore Roosevelt, Jr., but still did not like what he saw. General Pershing blamed General William Sibert, and sharply criticized him in front of Sibert's own staff.

In an interview with Forrest C. Pogue, Marshall said, "He was very severe with General Sibert...in front of all the officers. Among other things, he said that we didn't show any signs of much training; we had not justified the time we had had . . .and generally, he just scarified us. He didn't give General Sibert a chance to talk at all."

The criticisms embarrassed General Sibert and made George C. Marshall angry. Marshall felt the errors in the demonstration were his fault since he had made the plans. In front of everyone, as Pershing had done, Captain Marshall spoke up to Pershing in defense of General Sibert, trying to explain what had happened. That was Marshall's mistake. Pershing tried to ignore Marshall's comments and started to walk away. That was Pershing's mistake.

Without worrying about what the outcome might be for himself, Marshall put his hand on the general's arm, stopped him, and insisted on talking to him, or rather, talking at him. Marshall had a quick temper. He could talk fast and hard, overcoming the target of his anger with pure facts. When he was angry and needed to say something, he was difficult to stop.

According to the report, Captain George C. Marshall told General John J. "Black Jack" Pershing, in so many words, that he (Pershing) was wrong. He told Pershing that it wasn't General Sibert's staff's fault the troops were not ready to fight, it was his own (Pershing's) staff's fault. George C. Marshall knew who he was talking to, and why he felt so strongly. He also knew he was already "in up to my neck," and he "might as well not try to float but to splash a little bit."

Col. Marshall, January 4, 1919
First Army Headquarters, Bar Sur Aube, France

The other officers, including General Sibert, were shocked by Marshall's behavior and figured he had just gotten himself fired from his job. They hurried to say good-bye to him! But Marshall had no regrets and he told them, "All I can see is that I might get field duty instead of staff duty, and certainly that would be a great success." Later, when asked about the incident, Marshall said, "I was just mad all over. I had a rather inspired moment."

Nothing bad came from his flare-up, however. General Pershing didn't mention the incident again. In fact, whenever he came around for inspections after that day, Pershing always asked to see Marshall. Instead of firing Captain Marshall, he talked with Marshall about the many problems of the First Division. By the summer of 1918 Marshall was promoted to colonel (temporary) and had a place on Pershing's staff.

While serving under General Sibert, Marshall drafted plans and wrote orders. He wanted every officer to know his assignment and to have enough equipment to get the job done. Marshall did important, behind-the-scenes work, but it was a desk job, not a front-line fighting job. His hard work as an operations officer paid off for him in promotions.

It had taken Marshall fourteen years to reach the rank of captain, but only fourteen months to be promoted to (temporary) major, lieutenant colonel, and full colonel. Wartime promotions were temporary, effective only until the war was over, but at least they allowed Marshall the power to get the most necessary jobs done, and done correctly.

In *George C. Marshall, a General for Peace*, Alan Saunders wrote, "One of the many factors that made him a superb staff officer was his unwillingness to accept hearsay as fact. . . . He would venture to the front to see for himself. He was even cited for bravery under fire. More relevant though, was his willingness to learn, to listen to the comments and experience of (front) line officers, to fit orders to field conditions."

He would talk to the officers in charge of the fighting troops to get ideas on what they needed, where and when, and how they thought the best way to do things might be. Moving great numbers of men along with their supplies, food, and weapons was not easy.

His skill at organizing and directing the work, seeing the problems as well as the solutions, and managing other officers, made him valuable to the American forces. Still, George C. Marshall wanted to be a general, and not a temporary one, either. He was frustrated that he was not seeing active combat. He felt that commanding battle forces was one sure way to top-level ranking. Others of his age and experience were doing so. In June of 1918, he wrote to General Robert L. Bullard, asking to be assigned to active fighting and to have troop command.

Marshall's request was not granted. General Bullard wrote back that he felt Marshall's vital strength was in staff work, not on the battlefield. Marshall's superior officers knew his talent was too valuable to risk losing him on the front line of command. They needed him in the head offices, so they just gave him more work, but at a higher level! He was assigned to Pershing's GHQ (general headquarters) in the summer of 1918.

At the GHQ, he worked closely with Colonel Fox Conner. Marshall and Conner were at the center of planning and directing two of the biggest assaults against the German army. One was the Meuse-Argonne offensive, an attack involving the American, French, and Italian armies. Marshall figured out how to withdraw French and Italian soldiers and replace them with American forces without alerting the Germans.

In the middle of the important St. Mihiel battle, Marshall directed the movement of 220,000 men out of the front line and had 600,000 men moved into it, moving 3,000 guns (cannons) and 900,000 tons of supplies and ammunition by three rail lines and three roads. All movements were done at night, through the rain and mud and miserably cold weather, in order to maintain secrecy, With men and supplies both going and coming, moving out and moving in continually, the troops shifted places and reinforced each other.

A six-week, uninterrupted offensive against the Germans was maintained starting on September 26, 1918 and lasting until early November. By the time it was completed, about 1,200,000 American soldiers were involved. Marshall's planning was original, difficult and completely successful.

Mark Stoler writes, 'The Meuse-Argonne offensive was . . .a huge, complex, and extremely difficult operation . . . Marshall's planning was a logistical feat of unprecedented proportions, and it succeeded brilliantly."

Because of the relentless pounding of the allied forces, the German Army was worn down, beaten, and had to retreat. Germany surrendered and the guns fell silent. The Armistice was signed on the 11th hour of the 11th day of the 11th month, and the (First) World War was ended.

The American people called that first world war, 'The Great War', and at that time it was. From the ordinary soldier's point of view, there wasn't much great about it, except the miserable conditions, the confusion of the fighting, and the terrible loss of lives. America lost 53,500 men in combat. About 63,000 died of disease or accidents, and at least 200,000 were injured. George C. Marshall was one of the 1,432 officers and enlisted VMI men, aged seventeen to forty, who served in the Great War.

For the first few months after the World War ended, George C. Marshall acted as a supervisor of the clean-up crew of France and the U.S.Army. His main job involved keeping almost two million men out of trouble, helping to ready most of them for returning to America, and settling the remainder into an army of occupation, planned for maintaining the hard-earned peace.

In the early spring of 1919, there were celebrations to attend and honors to receive. He went with General Pershing and his staff to Metz where they were awarded the French Leigon of Honor medal for distinguished service. As they were marching, the man next to Marshall, Colonel James L. Collins, said, while staying in step, "How would you like to be the general's aide?"

It was an important question and Marshall made a quick, but important, decision for himself. He knew the change would mean more office work and no troop command, but he also knew, as aide-de-camp, he would be an adviser, and assistant to the most important general in the United States Army. That could not hurt his career very much.

From Metz, they went to Paris where the President of France reviewed (watched a formal parade) the troops. On Bastille Day, July 14, an official French holiday, Pershing and his staff joined a victory parade, leading the remaining American Expeditionary Force in the celebration. Crowds of French citizens cheered and waved along the streets, and 'a thousand lame, mutilated, and blind veterans' led the entire procession of important generals, other officers, and selected soldiers.

Col. George C. Marshall felt more sad than happy as he rode, remembering that the French nation had taken the brunt of the fighting and destruction. "As long as I live, I will never forget the faces I saw that day, because France was the actual battlefield. I don't suppose there was a single person there who had not lost someone dear."

That was only part of the victory celebration. From Paris, General Pershing and his staff went to London for a parade. Marshall remembered that day vividly because of the "devil of a horse" he had to ride. General Marshall told this story:

"Our horses were furnished by the English Army . . . I picked out a nice quiet looking one, and found him most satisfactory. We mounted and rode about a mile," Marshall said. But a General Brewster, had a large and unruly horse, and "I turned over my quiet animal to him and undertook the riding of his horse. The crowd was dense along the entire line of march and tremendously enthusiastic — all of which did not add to the peace of mind of my animal.

"For eight miles I had the ride of my life, and the worst phase of the trouble was that the horse tried to kick everything in reach . . . .the horse did not pull very hard, but he endeavored to go sidewise, and each time I straightened him out, he would rear. In going through the small passageway of the (Admiralty) Arch, I was forced to keep him straight, because women and children were jammed in close, and he would have killed a few . . . as the result of my straightening him out, he reared . . . lost his footing and went over backwards . . .

"As it turned out, I entered the Arch on a horse, and came out of it on a horse and did not even lose my place in the line-up, but I lost my temper for the rest of the ride." George C. Marshall was very grateful to get past the reviewing stand and off of that horse, with only one small broken bone in one hand.

The American officers spent a week in England celebrating the Armistice, and were entertained with banquets and parties given by the king and queen, and other royalty members. Upon returning to France, they enjoyed still more parades and celebrations in the villages. With General Pershing leading, they toured the battlefields and cemeteries where Americans had fought and were buried. Then they toured Italy and the battlefields there as well as Venice, Treviso, Vicenza, Milan and Turin and were guests of King Victor in Rome.

Alan Saunders wrote this about George C. Marshall: "What polish he might have lacked, he quickly acquired. He was also to see how power works at the highest circles. The men and the views he met during this period would stand him in good stead, for 20 years later he would face the same men or their successors either as enemies or allies."

On September 1, 1919, General John J. Pershing and his staff, including George C. Marshall, sailed for America on board the *Leviathan*. While still at sea, they received word that Congress had created and awarded the highest possible army rank, General of the Armies, with four stars, to General Pershing. George C. Marshall, was happy for him, but was left wondering about his own status of ranking.

He had gone to France as a captain, advanced to (temporary) major, lieutenant colonel, and colonel and was returning to Washington again, as a (permanent) captain. However, he went as an operations officer, but returned as an aide-de-camp (an assistant), to the top-ranking general of the entire army. Being Pershing's assistant was one of Marshall's longest army assignments and the one assignment that most helped prepare him for his own turn at the head of the Army, twenty years later.

Their ship docked in New York City harbor on the 8th of September, and Lily was there to meet him. On September 10, 1919, Marshall rode with the two other aides just behind General Pershing, and in front of the First Division men, in a ticker-tape victory parade, as the people welcomed the American Expeditionary Forces home to America and to New York City.

George and Lily Marshall
New York, 1920

From New York, they went by train to Philadelphia for a similar, but smaller, parade. Then, from Philadelphia to Washington, D.C. and down Pennsylvania Avenue, where thousands of people lined the streets, went the representatives of the victorious AEF.

George and Lily Marshall did not know it on that day, but they were home. With George working for General Pershing, whose office would be in the War Department, they would live in the city of Washington, D.C. for the next several years. They were back where they had started, in February of 1902, as newlyweds. They were home, for awhile.

General John J. Pershing and Col. George C. Marshall in France, 1919

Reporting for Duty

Chapter 8

People, Places, and Problems

September 1919 — October 1927

General John J. Pershing wanted George C. Marshall to be on his staff because, during the years in France, Marshall had taken on many responsibilities beyond his rank and shown exceptional leadership. He had developed in competence and ability. Pershing knew he could depend on Marshall to tell the truth, and to give helpful criticism if it was needed, even if it was not pleasant to hear. Although different in many ways, the two men were compatible and worked well together, and Marshall would add strength to Pershing's office.

Pershing was twenty years older, old enough to be Marshall's father. The two men had an understanding and appreciation of each other that allowed them to remain loyal friends for many years.

Both Marshall and Pershing had strong egos, and both were militarily ambitious. At West Point, Pershing had been an average student but was the top ranking cadet in his class every year just as Marshall had been at Virginia Military Institute. Both were known to be aloof, reserved, quick thinkers, and carefully professional in their actions. Both had strong and forceful tempers, as well as a good sense of humor. And both were sometimes disappointed with the army's slow rate of promotion, especially for George C. Marshall.

Even though Marshall was happy to be working with the great general, he was unhappy with his ranking status. Promotions still depended on older officers retiring and the Army needing replacement officers. If the Army was not enlarged, why would new officers be needed, even when older officers retired?

The officers who had just been through the tough times in France were convinced that the United States should maintain an army and not be caught again without trained forces and enough equipment. With Captain Marshall to help him prepare statistics and statements, General Pershing testified to Congress on the needs and reasons to maintain an army of about three hundred thousand. In June of 1920, Congress passed a bill that reorganized the U.S.Army, provided for maintenance of a peacetime army of 297,800 officers and men that could be called into action, but only if needed.

Marshall worked hard as General Pershing's busy assistant. Pershing was in great demand for giving speeches and making personal appearances, and he enjoyed traveling. Marshall took on more and more of the office duties, even letter writing, for the General. He stayed in contact, also with the VMI officials. They were hopeful of getting him to return to his alma mater as commandant of cadets, a teacher of military science, or even as superintendent, someday.

In June of 1920, Marshall convinced Pershing to travel with him to Lexington for a VMI visit, and to speak to the cadets. Marshall thought that hearing the highest ranking Army general and leader of the AEF speak would be impressive for cadets who might be considering a service career. Also, Marshall wanted General Pershing, a West Point graduate, to see the VMI he had heard of so often. While in Lexington, he took Pershing to visit the graves of two other great generals, also West Point graduates, Robert E. Lee and Stonewall Jackson.

On July 1, 1920 George C. Marshall was promoted to major, Regular Army, permanently. Warren G. Harding was elected president in November of 1920, and General John J. Pershing became the Army's chief of staff in July of 1921. During the next three years, Major Marshall "learned the ropes" in chief of staff work, in all areas. He sat in on meetings between Pershing and President Harding, wrote and sometimes gave speeches for the Chief of Staff. He prepared General Pershing with information, was beside him and ready with answers, whenever Pershing testified before Congress concerning military issues.

Marshall took on more and more of Pershing's duties, especially since the General traveled frequently. When Pershing vacationed in

France, once being away for six months, Marshall filled in for him completely. Marshall learned a great deal about the workings of politics and government. His steady and competent work paid off, for another promotion came through in August of 1923, when Marshall was promoted to lieutenant colonel.

One good part about working in Pershing's office was that Colonel Marshall could live in Washington, and so Lily came to live there, too. They had an apartment, near Pershing's office building, at 2400 Sixteenth Street. Finally, after being married eighteen years, they were able to settle down and make a home together again.

Lily enjoyed living in the city. She liked to shop and socialize with other officers' wives. Sadly, due to Lily's health problems, George C. Marshall never had children of his own. He was fond of children, enjoyed their company, and talking with them. Luckily, one day a little girl entered their lives.

In the same apartment building with the Marshalls, lived the Thomas Walker Page family. Rose Page was eight years old when she met Colonel Marshall one day in the elevator. Beginning then and lasting for the next forty years, she and George C. Marshall shared a deep, adult-child, father-daughter type of friendship. Rose was an out-spoken and out-going child whose personality delighted both Marshalls.

Rose often ate dinner in their apartment or with them in the dining room of the apartment house. They took her on picnics and walks, or on outings in their Model T Ford, even traveling to Lexington to visit Lily's mother. She became the daughter they never had for themselves, and Rose Page chose the Marshalls to be her godparents when she was confirmed in her church.

Rose Page grew up, married, and had children. She had long-lasting memories and impressions of the Marshalls, and she wrote a book, *General Marshall Remembered*, published in 1968, about her experiences with them. Her book is a collection of stories about the Marshalls and offers a view of George C. Marshall that few others ever saw. In an interview about her book, Rose Page Wilson said that General Marshall displayed the same qualities in his private life that he did in his professional life— integrity, patience, toler-ance and understanding. She said that he taught her fairness, honesty, and forgiveness, as well as how to ride a horse. She wanted her children to learn from George C. Marshall, too.

She said that Marshall's "principles might seem prudish by ordinary standards, but they were fundamental rules rooted deeply in his uncomplicated Christian faith and supported by his incorruptible honor." Marshall was not a saint by any means, but he lived by high principles.

Rose learned from Lily, too. She thought Lily was a kind and beautiful lady, just as Colonel Marshall did, and she wrote, "He showered Lily with a hundred little attentions. He fetched and carried. He planned little surprises. He was ever solicitous about her health and comfort." Lily once told Rose, "George just naturally has to look after me. It's his pleasure, bless his heart. You too. Haven't you noticed how he absolutely has to take care of us fragile females?"

Colonel Marshall was quite fond of Rose Page, enjoyed entertaining her and watching her learn. He was always interested in her struggles, her successes, her thoughts and adventures. He even wrote verses for her, like this one:

1. A little girl I strive to please
   Is very shy and loves to tease
   And tell all kinds of funny jokes
   About all kinds of curious folks.
2. She likes to ride and dance and coast
   But better still to butter toast
   And smear it deep with honey sweet
   And sit and eat and eat and eat

3. I think that some time in the spring
   She'l (sic) eat so much of everything
   Her dresses all will spread and split
   And open out to make a fit.
4. And then perhaps she'l look right thin
   With strips of dress and streaks of skin
   I think she'l look read odd like that
   With nothing whole except her hat.

In 1924, when General Pershing retired from the Army, George C. Marshall put in a request for a new assignment, one he had wanted for some time, with the Fifteenth Infantry in China, and with troops for him to command. After his orders came through, George and Lily took Lily's mother with them, left Washington, D.C. and Rose Page behind.

Setting sail July 12, out of New York on the *U.S.A.T. St. Mihiel*, and after stops in Panama, San Francisco and Honolulu, they arrived on Sunday, September 7, in Tientsin (ten-sen) China.

George C. Marshall wrote to Pershing from China, "Altogether I find things very interesting. The regiment has select personnel for officers, and it is a pleasure to work with them. But I must confess that I have a hard time realizing that everything I do is not being done directly for you. My five years with you will always remain the unique experience of my career . . . Not until I took up these new duties . . . did I realize how much my long association was going to mean to me and how deeply I will miss it."

George C. Marshall wrote to a friend who had been with him on General Pershing's staff, General John L. Hines: "I am more and more pleased with my choice of station and duty. It suits me perfectly, and the most disagreeable duty here is preferable to desk duty."

Marshall fully enjoyed his three-year tour of duty in China. He found his job less tedious than working in an office all the time for he enjoyed working with the soldiers, meeting other officers, training a horse, and learning Chinese. He wrote from China to General Pershing: "I have done my best to perfect myself in Chinese and last week caught up with the first class to start Chinese instruction in February, 1924. "At my present rate I should be well ahead of them in another month . . . .."

He set about learning the language, determined to learn it faster than any other officer. He was not required to speak the language, he simply wanted to learn it, and so he did, mastering a two-year course in only eleven months. Nevertheless, he made mistakes in speaking Chinese, to the Chinese people, now and then.

One day Marshall needed his Chinese chauffeur to bring the car around. When he spoke in Chinese, asking for the car, the chauffeur did not understand. George C. Marshall requested his car again only louder, and the man still did not understand. Marshall said the same phrase again, without any luck, finally gave up, and just said, "Oh, hell! Send my car!" And the car was brought around promptly!

Then Marshall noticed the regimental chaplain who had watched and overheard the whole exchange. "You heard?" Marshall asked. "Yes," said the chaplain. "Will it go all over the Army?" Marshall asked. The Chaplain answered, "Yes, sir, it *will* go all over the Army."

For relaxation, George C. Marshall trained and rode a Mongolian pony, a horse somewhat smaller than a regular horse.

Col. Marshall trained and rode a Mongolian pony while in China 1924-27.

He wrote to General John L. Hines: "I have finally trained a Mongolian pony up into a delightful riding animal and do eight to twelve miles every morning, and at least one mile at top speed on the race course. Sundays, of course, I get in twenty or twenty-five miles, so it is much like our riding program at Myer. The past month, tennis has occupied my attention in the late afternoon. The American Tennis Club is convenient and delightfully sociable."

In a letter to General Pershing, Marshall reported, "I grow more and more satisfied with service in China . . . They (the officers) do a tremendous amount of athletics — soccer, rugby, and American football, basket and base ball, ice hockey, field sports, boxing and wrestling."

While George was busy learning Chinese, training his Mongolian pony and playing tennis or squash, Lily and her mother went shopping. Chinese goods were plentiful and inexpensive for Americans in China, and would be highly prized as souvenirs of their travels when they returned to the States. Servants were plentiful and inexpensive in China, also, for the officers' wives. Without household chores to do, because of the servants, Lily had plenty of shopping time.

Lily bought rugs, linens, silks, silver, dishes and other decorative items for the home she hoped to furnish, as well as exquisite clothes. George C. Marshall enjoyed seeing Lily so active and happily engaged. They had more time to be together than they had had in earlier years.

When Marshall completed his tour of duty, Lily's Chinese trophies, for her future home in the states, were carefully crated and put aboard the ship. The Marshalls and Lily's mother sailed in May, returning to the States in the early summer of 1927. They were headed for Washington, D.C. and Colonel Marshall's next assignment.

Along the way, Lily did not feel well. A slow, two-week drive from San Francisco to Lexington failed to emotionally energize her, or to increase her physical strength. After leaving Lily's mother in Lexington, and trying to settle into their own Washington routine, their lives soon took a sharp and distressing turn for the worse.

George C. Marshall's job was at the Army War College, where he was to lecture. He did not enjoy desk-type jobs, but he did enjoy teaching. Teaching was work that George C. Marshall found stimulating, and challenging. His experiences from Fort Leavenworth, the Great War, his stint with General Pershing, and his adventures in China would be valuable in his instruction of other officers.

According to Forrest C. Pogue, Marshall was "one of those rare teachers who make a difference, who open minds in such a way that they never afterward quite close again or forget the excitement of a new idea."

Lily looked forward to setting up a real home in the city and showing off some of their Chinese treasures in it. George C. Marshall would rather live in the country, but he loved Lily and if it pleased her to live in Washington, he would gladly work there. He hoped the city excitement would help restore her to good health. Even as George began his teaching, he tried to get Lily to rest, to recover from the illness that had left her so weak and frail. That did not happen.

In early August, Lily entered Walter Reed Hospital for treatment. During the medical examination, doctors found her thyroid gland had a goiter (tumor-like growth) growing, inward and down, into her chest. The goiter needed to be removed; she needed surgery. Lily was weak, but refused to eat, and the doctors refused to operate. She was sent home and her doctors made George personally responsible for overseeing her diet.

His job was to help her increase her strength, so she could be strong enough for the surgery. The Marshalls moved into a large house with white columns near the War College. They postponed the unpacking while George followed the doctors' orders and saw to Lily's diet. He was a doting husband and wanted to help her. In two weeks, she gained nine pounds!

She remained weak, though, because she had trouble eating. The goiter pressed against her esophagus making it hard to swallow, and breathing was difficult due to the pressure of the goiter on her trachea (windpipe). She returned to the hospital on August 21 and had the surgery the next day.

Lily's surgery took longer, and was more complicated, than expected. After the operation, George could not see her for thirty-six hours. She was in serious condition and was sedated with morphine. He was only allowed a few moments with her daily for the next five days. Then, her condition began to improve slowly but steadily, and she seemed on the road to recovery. She wrote a letter to her aunt and said, "I believe if I had had any notion beforehand I might not have had the courage to face it."

While Lily was in the hospital, George was teaching every day, and did very little to unpack or settle things into their new home. According to Lily's letters, George was "just sort of picnicking" among the crates and boxes. He visited her whenever he could, and she appreciated his visits immensely. She wrote, "George is so wonderful and helps me so. He puts heart and strength in me."

On the morning of September 15, 1927, the doctor told her she could go home the next day. She was excited and happy to hear that, and started a letter to her mother, telling her the good news. While writing, her weakened heart finally failed her. She slumped forward with pen in hand, and died. The last word she wrote was George.

Meanwhile, Marshall was in class at the War College. He was summoned to the telephone, spoke for a few moments, then put his head on his arms on the desk in absolute grief. A guard, on duty, asked if he could do anything for him. Marshall replied: "No, Mr.Throckmorton . . . I just had word my wife, who was to join me here today, has just died."

Lily's death sent George C. Marshall into a deep, soul-aching, painful time. He wandered numbly about the house. Lily had planned to decorate the house, making their first real home together. Now that she was gone, that home would never be made. He went to work, and tried to teach, but his heart was broken. He didn't know who to turn to, or what to do. He had no children or close friends to help fill the lonely hole that Lily's death had left in his life.

General Pershing wrote him a sympathy note to which George Marshall responded on October 14, 1927 in this way, "twenty-six years of most intimate companionship, something I have known ever since I was a mere boy, leaves me lost in my best efforts to adjust myself to future prospects in life. If I had been given to club life . . . with men outside of athletic diversions, or if there was a campaign (war) on or other pressing duty demanding a concentrated effort, then I think I could do better. However, I will find a way."

Marshall controlled his emotions so tightly that he showed no outward signs of grief. He did tell his goddaughter, Rose Page, who was then sixteen, "I'm so lonely, so lonely." Because Rose had loved Lily too, he gave her Lily's hand embroidered lingerie still packed in the sachet from China, strands of pearls, a fur stole, feather boas, and a Chinese silk wrap with billowing sleeves. He said, "She used to wear it serving tea. She always managed to reach for things so the butterfly sleeves would show."

He needed a change of scene, a new approach to life. What he really needed was a new job; one that would help him adjust to life without Lilly, one that would occupy his time fully. Luckily, his friends in charge of postings and assignments for Army officers understood his problem and came to his rescue.

Photo donated to the George C. Marshall Research Library by Lorraine Pitman.

Col. George C. Marshall at Woodville, Va. in 1927, after Lily died.

Lieutenant Colonel George C. Marshall, assistant commandant of the
Infantry School, Fort Benning, Georgia

Reporting for Duty

Chapter 9

About Face, By George!

November 1927 — June 1932

In November 1927, George C. Marshall became the assistant commandant of the Infantry School, a division of the Officers Training School, at Fort Benning, Georgia. The students at the Officers Training school were newly commissioned officers, as well as officers from the Reserves and the National Guard. Marshall was in charge of the Academic Department, which meant he could design the Infantry curriculum. The job was exactly what he needed — professional advancement, intensive work, and a remedy for his grief.

General Marshall told his official biographer, Forrest C. Pogue, "The change to Benning was magical . . . caught me at my most restless moment and gave me hundreds of interests, an unlimited field of activity, delightful associates, and all outdoors to play in."

Not only was the assignment good for him, but he did an important job for the Army. In bringing new ideas, adding new faculty, and changing the curriculum of the school, George C. Marshall was later credited with starting the "Benning Revolution." According to Pogue, "It was a happy circumstance that at his 'most restless moment' he was given a teaching job . . . with . . .the authority and scope to make a mark not only on the Infantry School but on the United States Army."

Marshall brought vital instruction and inspiration to the Infantry School at Fort Benning. He felt that if war should come again, the Infantry must be ready to move and attack quicker and with more skill. Faster weapons along with total training for their use must be taught.

Combat practice in the field at Fort Benning, Georgia, 1932.

(U.S. Army photograph)

Instruction that had once been given in the classroom was moved outside onto the firing range, or into the Georgia fields, to give the men 'hands-on experience.' Ed Cray wrote: "In just short of five years, Marshall managed to thoroughly revamp both the instructional style and the technical concepts taught the 150 lieutenants and captains in each year's class."

Over two hundred of "Marshall's Men", as they called themselves, who were either faculty or students during his five years at Fort Benning, served as generals in World War II.

Marshall not only brought changes to Fort Benning, but also to himself. The professional stress of his new position and increased social activities at Fort Benning, as well as his grief, endangered his health during the first years after Lily's death. He lost weight and developed problems with an irregular heartbeat and high blood pressure.

His doctor, Colonel Morrison C. Stayer, was concerned and afraid of a possible physical breakdown. He ordered George C. Marshall to make some personal changes, such as giving up cigarettes and scotch, and taking up happier, healthier habits like exercise. Marshall agreed to try. He was a chain smoker, and he did cut back on his smoking. Giving up alcohol did not bother him since he did not think it was proper for a soldier to drink during the prohibition era, when liquor was illegal, anyway. He enjoyed exercise, so he happily increased his outdoor activities.

Marshall believed in relaxation and exercise, and if one could combine the two, that was good. Daily swimming, tennis and early morning horseback riding became part of his routine. Although he preferred a quiet canter, he organized foxhunts for the officers and their wives, and let them do the weekly cross-country chasing of foxes. Night rides were organized for pairs of riders trying to reach certain points between start and finish, but free to go at it any way they wished. He participated in those, or he joined one of the exciting horseback treasure hunts he arranged for everyone. One favorite story from Fort Benning about George C. Marshall tells of his riding in from a treasure hunt, wearing a Japanese kimono, a Filipino hat, and carrying a birdcage.

He sometimes organized special parades for visitors to Fort Benning. Marshall found watching the normal troop review, with band-playing and marching, boring. The Marshall-style of review might have several acts, or different ways, for showing off the many activities of Fort Benning. His favorite pageant-like parades included officer students marching by carrying their weapons, followed by the tennis players with their rackets, polo players on their ponies, and the basketball and baseball players. The grand finale was sometimes a make-believe fox hunt complete with dogs running through the crowd and the hunters on horseback right behind them.

Colonel Marshall hosted dinner parties at his house, or often ate with friends. He enjoyed good food and conversation together. He became an entertaining storyteller and enjoyed telling long, involved, and even funny stories. Some of his stories had actually happened to himself or to someone he knew. Marshall had a keen sense of humor and liked to play practical jokes on his friends. He played Bridge with other officers or with couples and with his memory, he was probably tough to beat at card games. Although he seemed more sociable than he had been when Lily was alive, he was still reserved and formal and a hard person to get close to, unless it was his idea.

Stoler wrote "Usually an impressive individual with an overwhelming air of confidence and authority, he could also be a stuffed shirt and a prudish bore. He never told off-color stories, and could wither with a stare anyone who did." Some of Marshall's students nicknamed him 'Uncle George' because of his strict attention to details and directions, his fact-filled small talk, and his fatherly behavior toward them. They may have used the nickname when talking among themselves, but never where he could hear them!

In the two years after Lily died, both his mother and Lily's mother died. To help him from being too lonely, his sister Marie Singleton and Rose Page, his goddaughter, often visited with him in what he called, "the nicest one (house) I ever had." The Fort Benning house had lovely garden space, and Georgia climate had long growing seasons. George C. Marshall liked to garden, even as a boy, and found relaxation in working with plants. His sister Marie agreed the gardens were lovely, but thought the inside of the

George C. Marshall with department heads and instructors at the Infantry School, Fort Benning, Georgia, 1930-31. Front Row, left to right: Lt. Col. Morrison C. Stayer, Lt. Col. Joseph W. Stilwell, Lt. Col. Marshall, Major William F. Freehoff, Major Edwin F. Harding. Back row: Capt. Howard J. Liston, Major Omar N. Bradley, Major Emil W. Leand, First Lt. Fremont B. Hodson.

house seemed dreary, with too many pictures of Lily in every room. Whenever Marie visited, she quietly caused some of the pictures to 'disappear.'

George Marshall stayed busy and on the go, perhaps because he was lonely. Marshall enjoyed the company of many married friends, but he had decided never to marry again. He felt he could never find another Lily, and he did not. Instead he found a Katherine.

A new and different kind of woman came into Marshall's life in 1929 as the result of a small dinner party given at a friend's home. Colonel Marshall was introduced to Katherine Brown, who was a friend of Marshall's friends. The evening turned out to be a new beginning for both of them.

Katherine Tupper Brown, a daughter of a Kentucky Baptist minister, a former stage actress, and a widow with three teenage children, was visiting with friends in the nearby city of Columbus, Georgia. Mr. and Mrs. Tom Hudson invited her and Col. Marshall for dinner one evening. Having been a widow for just over a year, Mrs. Brown seldom went out socially because she didn't think it was correct to socialize so soon after her husband's death.

When Katherine arrived at the Hudsons' home, she went into the living room where she first saw George C. Marshall, standing in front of the fireplace. In her book, *Together*, Katherine Marshall wrote, "My first impression was of a tall, slender man with sandy hair and deep-set eyes. I will never forget . . . George had a way of looking right through you. He had such keen blue eyes and he was straight and very military."

During dinner, the two talked comfortably with each other, swapping funny stories. Mrs. Brown was quite interested in this unusual army officer. When it was time to go home from the dinner party, George Marshall asked if he might drive Mrs. Brown to Mrs. William Blanchard's house where she was visiting. Mrs. Brown agreed to let him.

They drove around and around the streets of Columbus for about an hour. Finally, Katherine Brown asked the colonel how long he had been at Fort Benning and he told her two years. Katherine Brown then asked, "After two years, haven't you learned your way around Columbus?"

Katherine Tupper Brown Marshall

"Extremely well," George C. Marshall replied, " or I could not have stayed off the block (street) where Mrs. Blanchard lives."

Katherine's husband had been a lawyer in Baltimore, who was murdered by an unhappy client. The attractive Katherine Brown, tall and dark-haired, had grieved for her husband, and so had George Marshall, for Lily. Suddenly, for both of them, it was time for a change. "He was as smitten as a sober man of forty-eight might be" wrote Ed Cray.

George C. Marshall and Katherine Tupper Brown were married on October 15, 1930 at the Emmanuel Episcopal Church in Baltimore, Maryland. General John J. Pershing was Marshall's best man. It was a small wedding with a limited number of people, but when the news got out that General Pershing was there a crowd formed outside the church to greet the wedding party. The Marshalls did not mind sharing their day with General Pershing's fans, but they did not linger there.

From the ceremony they went right to the train and straight back to Fort Benning. Katherine Marshall learned to be a colonel's wife and George C. Marshall learned to be a stepfather. At last, he had a family! Marshall did not adopt the children or change their names, their last name was Brown and Brown it remained. Molly and Clifton, the two oldest children called him "the Colonel" but Allen, the youngest and closest to Marshall, was one of the few people ever to call him "George".

As Lily Marshall had been weak and inactive, Katherine Marshall was the opposite, being healthy and strong, and fond of the out of doors. She was an 'About Face' in wives for George C. Marshall! His love for Lily was forever strong, but so was his friendly, comfortable, and secure love for Katherine. Life at Fort Benning turned out to be happier than George C. Marshall had expected, and Katherine was partly responsible for that. However, Army life is always changing, and nothing stays the same for very long.

Reporting for Duty

Chapter 10

North Beyond Benning

June 30, 1932 —- October 1, 1936

After four and a half years at Fort Benning, in the spring of 1932, George C. Marshall was assigned to command a battalion of the Eighth Infantry at Fort Screven, Georgia, near Savannah. He was pleased with the assignment and especially glad to be back with troops. Fort Screven had less than 400 men, but Marshall wrote to General Pershing that even if the post was small, it kept him, ". . . out of doing just office work."

During his stay at Fort Screven, Marshall began reaching out to the general public and making connections with civilians. The base was ten miles from the city, but the Marshalls attended an Episcopal church there, became friends with the mayor, and joined the Chamber of Commerce. Marshall thought it was important to let the people know the Army was not their enemy, although their personal taxes paid the Army bills.

Fort Screven was smaller and rather shabby compared to Fort Benning, and Marshall knew that money for repairs was tight. One of the younger officers wrote that Marshall took over the post, "as would a Southern planter his domain." He was a stickler for details, and during his morning rides, he looked for things that needed fixing, then assigned someone to do it. He and Mrs. Marshall worked at sprucing up their own yard by planting and weeding, and soon other officers and their families were out in their yards, doing the same.

One area of Marshall's leadership was not exactly with army troops, but with the Civilian Conservation Corps. In November of 1932, Franklin D. Roosevelt was elected to be the 32nd President of the United States. The Great Depression was underway, causing widespread poverty in the nation. Millions of men were out of work, the general economy was in terrible trouble and families were hungry. Ten days after his inauguration, President Roosevelt, who valued the environment, started the Civilian Conservation Corps, as part of his New Deal program.

The CCC was designed to give jobs and training to thousands of unemployed young men. Camps were set up around the nation and young men between 17 and 25 were taken out of the cities and from the farms where they had no jobs and put to work. They were given safe housing, three meals a day, and a salary of $30 a month in return for their labor. They could keep five dollars but the rest was sent home to their families.

Roosevelt directed the CCC toward repair and conservation of natural resources. Its members cleared trails, fought fires, built campgrounds, bridges, dams, roads, and planted trees. Evidence of their work is still visible today in national parks, national forests, and national roads, such as the Blue Ridge Parkway.

The Forrest Service and the Soil Conservation Service were called on to direct the work, but to use the Army for help. Because the work required equipment and organization, the U.S. Army was used to outfit, equip, and oversee the basic care of the men. Since the Army was required to oversee the organizing and building of the camps, commanding officers from bases in each area were responsible for directing the work. That is how George C. Marshall became involved with the CCC.

Marshall was assigned to inspect and report on the nineteen camps being built in eastern Georgia and Florida. He believed in the CCC idea from the beginning, and gave his wholehearted support in getting the camps set up and running. He enjoyed being personally involved in organizing the camps.

Colonel Marshall attended the opening of each new camp, making it as much of a celebration as possible. He visited and inspected the camps under his control regularly, making sure the camps were clean and orderly, and that the men received good medical and dental care. He arranged reading and writing lessons for those who needed them. He became acquainted with the men and encouraged their learning to fish, swim, and sail.

He enjoyed his assignment at Fort Screven, but only a year later, in June of 1933, he was sent to Fort Moultrie, South Carolina, near Charleston. There he commanded the Eighth Infantry Regiment and supervised fifteen South Carolina CCC camps. His promotion to full colonel became official on September 1, 1933.

Whenever George C. Marshall moved to a new post, he started his job as Mrs. Marshall wrote, ". . .with the enthusiasm of a young lieutenant on his first assignment. . . No detail was too small for his attention, no soldier too lowly for his interest. . . He seemed to put as much thought into the personal welfare of his men as he put into their military training."

Ft. Moultrie, too, needed a bit of sprucing up, Marshall thought. Wherever he noticed a base building that needed repairing or a paint brush, he quickly ordered it done. Trees and shrubs were planted to brighten up the grounds.

But sadly, in some ways, Congress cut the funds for the armed forces, including officers pay. Times were hard everywhere. Katherine Marshall wrote, "These were lean, depression years. In order that the men could manage to feed their families on their small pay, my husband personally supervised the building of chicken yards, and hog pens and the planting of vegetable gardens,.

Marshall started a lunch pail system whereby the men could get a good, hot dinner, cooked at the mess, to take home to their families at a very small cost." A soldier's entire family, regardless of size, could have the same hot meal he did for ten or fifteen cents a day. Mrs. Marshall remembered, "We ate this mid-day dinner ourselves until the custom was well established—so that he might know what the men were getting. It saved their wives endless toil that hot summer, a godsend to the married enlisted personnel."

Marshall enjoyed his work at Fort Moultrie including the setting up and supervising of his assigned CCC camps. Katherine often went with him on the inspection trips, and always went to an opening. She said, "For hours we stood that summer, under the burning South Carolina sun on little pinewood platforms, hastily erected, so that he might be present at the raising of the flag over the new CCC camp."

He was completely intent and happy in his work, expecting to spend at least two years at Fort Moultrie. Then, all of a sudden, things changed! To say the least, he was surprised, if not shocked, when in October of 1933, he was transferred to Chicago to become the senior instructor of the Illinois National Guard. The National Guard, even though it was highly thought of by many state politicians, was still considered to be a place to hide the less able and ineffective officers. The National Guard was not part of the Regular Army and certainly not the road to becoming a general.

In Marshall's opinion, Chicago was a demotion. He had been close to zeroing in on his first general's star, then suddenly he was sent backwards down the ladder of promotion by being taken away from troop command. Marshall's career would go nowhere if he had no troops and, just as bad, he would have to leave the CCC camps to someone else. It just did not seem fair.

For the first time in his army career, he wrote a letter to the Army Chief of Staff, General Douglas MacArthur, asking for a reconsideration, to be given another assignment. General Pershing even wrote to MacArthur on Marshall's behalf. The letters did no good. The orders stood, and the orders were obeyed. The Marshalls moved to Chicago.

Katherine Marshall wrote, "Those first months in Chicago I shall never forget. George had a gray, drawn look which I had never seen before and have seldom seen since." Rose Page came to visit and asked when he would become chief of staff, and Marshall told her, "Well, Rosie, it looks now as if I never will. If I don't make brigadier general soon, I'll be so far behind in seniority I won't even be in the running."

The Marshalls' apartment was a thirty - minute walk from the National Guard headquarters in the Loop of Chicago, and the walk became Marshall's exercise of the day. The National Guard, being made up of civilians who train on weekends and in the summers, had enough of the military flavor to hold his interest and provided contact with the civilian population. Somehow, he made the needed adjustments to his life once again. He put his heart and soul into working with the Illinois National Guard, turning things around for their division and for himself.

Colonel Marshall with National Guard members, Chicago, 1934

Forrest C. Pogue wrote, "Marshall's extraordinary zest and energy made him take his disappointments hard. . . Yet the same zest and energy made it impossible for him to remain long in a state of depression." Marshall loved dogs, and one way to lift his spirits was to get an Irish Setter puppy. He named the pup Pontiac, and walked with him daily among the vacant lots near the apartment building.

Once again Marshall taught by setting forth both orders and example. He reminded the 33rd Division men that the War Department would not respect their unit or recognize it unless they shaped up, and did things right. He taught them what to do, gave them a challenge, made them proud of their unit again. He soon saw improvement in their training, and his three-year assignment was successful.

From Pogue's *Education of a General*, we can read, "it is obvious he caused a 'flurry of excitement' in the Chicago National Guard with his well-tailored uniform and shiny boots, a lean, tall, straight figure whose cold blue and seldom smiling eyes could make a man feel singularly silly and superfluous — a self-possessed officer who asked hard questions in his soft voice . . . the manner was not put on for effect. The colonel was a taskmaster who in drill demanded smartness, promptness, and precision —the head-high military snap — and exact obedience to orders."

Always in the background, Marshall stayed in touch with General Pershing and they frequently exchanged letters. General Pershing kept hoping that he could help push Marshall into position for his promotion to general, but he did not seem able to do so. Seniority was the rule of promotions, and there were only a limited number of positions available each year, as older officers retired. George C. Marshall would just have to wait his turn.

Reporting for Duty

Chapter 11

A Great Northwest Adventure

October 1936 – July 1938

George C. Marshall's turn to be a general came when he was fifty-eight years old, after spending thirty-six years in the army. On October 1, 1936, he officially became a brigadier general, and put his first star on his uniform.

Along with the promotion came his orders to a new post, commanding the Fifth Brigade of the Third Infantry Division at Vancouver Barracks in the state of Washington. The post was in the city of Vancouver, just across the state line from Portland, Oregon and a long, long way from Chicago.

His new assignment was good because he would be with Regular Army again. The 5th Brigade had regiments stationed in eastern Washington, Montana, North Dakota and Alaska, and Marshall's job was to visit their posts and inspect the troops on a regular basis. He was also assigned to supervise the twenty-five Civilian Conservation Corps camps in that district. He remembered opening the CCC camps of Georgia and South Carolina several years before, and was keenly interested to see how those in the Pacific Northwest compared. He was happy and eager to get started on both jobs.

A new rank and a new assignment meant a new car! Their old Ford was almost worn out and the Marshalls wanted to drive from Chicago to Vancouver. After some careful shopping, he brought home a brand new touring sedan, a Packard 120, from an Oak Park, Illinois agent. George C. Marshall paid about a thousand dollars for it!

Then, the General, proudly driving at about 30 mph, Mrs. Marshall, and her daughter, Molly, took a three-week trip West. Along the way, he had his car serviced every five hundred miles or so. They had car trouble only once, but that once cost them extra time and almost ten dollars to repair!

Otherwise, General Marshall, a lover of history, filled their travel time with Indian and Western stories and facts he had learned from his father, as a boy in Pennsylvania. All three enjoyed the sightseeing and the leisure of their vacation. Pontiac, the General's dog, traveled to Vancouver by train. The Marshalls arrived at Vancouver Barracks on October 27, 1936.

Marshall was pleasantly surprised to find Colonel Henry Hossfeld, commanding officer of the Seventh Infantry, there to welcome him and shake his hand. They had served together in the Philippines, when they were both lieutenants. Mrs. Marshall wrote, "George had telegraphed ahead that he wished to enter the post quietly, with no ceremonies, but when we reached the entrance of Vancouver Barracks the band and a Guard of Honor was waiting at the gate."

Pontiac was there, with an orderly holding his leash. The men and officers stood at attention, and the official post band played. When Marshall stepped from the car to acknowledge the salute, Pontiac saw his master.

Katherine Marshall wrote, "He gave one leap, broke the leash and landed square on George's chest, all but knocking him down. Then he ran like mad in and out of the formation, jumping up on the soldiers, throwing his whole body first against one and then another. He completely disrupted the ceremony." Colonel Hossfeld was a "very military man and there was murder in his eye... anyone could see he would gladly have thrown Ponty into the Columbia River. He did not realize that such a welcome from his dog meant more to George Marshall than any formal reception that could have been given him."

As commander of an important army post, Marshall became a meaningful member of the entire community. Another friend of his earlier Army days, retired General Charles H. Martin, was then governor of Oregon. He introduced the new general to other significant and influential civilians. The General developed friendly ties, both personally and officially, with political and business leaders, and he enjoyed being involved in various community activities, especially the Chamber of Commerce.

Marshall was a popular speaker for community organizations. He was not a serious speaker, but more of a storyteller. He talked about people or places, the CCC, and especially the Army and his experiences in it. His stories were sometimes funny, usually full of information, and always entertaining. By the end of his first year, and after many dinner meetings, he said he was "talking for my supper" much too often.

The Marshalls' house on Officers Row, was about a hundred years old, spacious, and historic. Civil War generals had lived in it, too. The house faced the Vancouver Barracks parade ground and the mountains. From her bedroom window, Mrs. Marshall could see the snow-capped top of Mt. Hood in the distance. There were sixty varieties of roses, a colorful dahlia bed, and fruit trees in the Marshalls' yard to care for, much to his delight. As a hobby and for relaxation, Marshall always enjoyed gardening.

In his work, Marshall was happily back with Infantry troops and the CCC. He was always busy. Both Marshalls enjoyed fishing and, when they did not have dinner parties to attend or guests to care for, they often grabbed their frying pan and headed out to fish for their supper on the Lewis or Columbia rivers, a lake, or a stream near the post. They caught their supper and cooked it near the water. Sometimes they took Pontiac for long walks in the evergreen woods near their house. They later referred to their time in Vancouver as their "happiest two years" in the Army.

But life is seldom perfect, and Marshall had at least one significant time of trouble during those two years, and it came in the first few months. One of his old health problems, his irregular heart rate, returned to worry him. At Fort Benning, his doctor had diagnosed the cause of his rapid and irregular pulse. His thyroid gland was not working right. For a few years after Fort Benning, the condition did not bother him, but just before leaving Chicago, it started acting up again. After arriving in Vancouver, it became worse.

His heart rate would be regular at seventy-two beats per minute then leap to ninety or one hundred, with no reason. He was quick to lose his temper, easily irritated and often grouchy. He did not

George C. Marshall was promoted to brigadier general
on October 1, 1936.

feel ill, but he definitely had a problem. Marshall was worried that word of his illness would get around the Army, and that his position at Vancouver Barracks might be threatened. The army chief of staff, at the War Department in Washington, D.C., might replace him if he thought Marshall was not physically fit. Surgery was needed his doctors said.

In December of 1936, he went to the Army's Letterman Hospital in San Francisco where he stayed for five weeks. First off, he caught the flu, which was a help in one way, since it kept him confined to bed. He had to recover from that before any other treatment could begin. He decided to have the operation, and to do his best to get well. A diseased and enlarged part of his thyroid gland was removed. He was a good patient, obeyed the doctors orders, and all went well.

Surgery was the answer! Afterwards, his heart rate dropped back to normal, and he soon recovered from the operation. It wasn't long before everyone noticed that Marshall's bad temper and irritability were not as quick and strong as they had been. He was relatively calm about things, and with everybody, which was much better for him and everyone around him.

Marshall wanted his recovery to remain successful. He learned how to carefully monitor his pulse for himself. He completely quit smoking and began regular exercise routines. To his daily morning horseback rides he added hunting, fishing, tennis, and a little bit of golf whenever he could. Any rumors that he was not physically fit were soon squelched, and his job remained secure. He was soon able to do again what he enjoyed doing most—organizing places and men. His plan of attack for those battles needed weapons of a different kind.

For starters, he designed several new training policies for the men of Vancouver Barracks, and directed the methods for putting them into practice. One objective was to increase the number of new enlisted men, and during his tenure, the Barracks had its highest re-enlistment rate in years. Second, since the buildings and grounds on post were in great need of repair, he went after permission and money to spruce up Vancouver Barracks.

Marshall wrote letters to the War Department, the state senators and representatives, and the two state governors, asking money to help with every phase of repair and rebuilding. He presented his case well, and the money came through. The much needed chopping, digging and planting, hammering and sawing, and the swishing of paintbrushes began.

By the time he left, over $400,000 had been spent on post improvements. Marshall's campaigns, to improve both the military routines and the physical environment, had a positive impact on the people living on or near the army base.

Along with the technical and environmental sides of training, George C. Marshall cared about the personal life of his troops. He made sure physical, recreational, and social life were not neglected, and he kept close tabs on the soldiers' families, as well as the men themselves. He knew many of the 1,600 soldiers who lived on or near the army post by name. One of the places that received some attention, with Marshall's help, was the post chapel.

General Marshall was a solid Episcopalian, and believed in the value of worship. Marshall was glad the soldiers had a chapel to attend, although it was in an abandoned warehouse. Soon after he arrived, he attended chapel services conducted by the post chaplain, Captain Martin C. Poch. The chapel was bare and cold, with only a hand-made wooden cross on a makeshift altar. Not many soldiers attended services, either. George C. Marshall was concerned, and so was the chaplain.

Captain Poch wished the chapel had shiny brass candlesticks and a cross for the altar, like some regular churches. He knew the budget could provide no money to brighten up an old warehouse-chapel. After all, the Great Depression was still in full swing. But the captain had a plan. He told it to General Marshall who liked Poch's idea, gave his approval, and helped put it into action.

Soon the VB (Vancouver Barracks) men were asked by Captain Poch to go out around the post, on a treasure hunt of sorts. They were to look for old brass; anything made from brass that was not in use. The soldiers knew that one of the easiest places to find used brass was at the rifle range. They collected empty shells and cartridge casings after every firing practice.

The men also brought in brass shoulder ornaments and belt buckles from old uniforms, along with brass souvenirs collected during their travels. Some of the oldest buildings on the post were being remodeled, and the men brought in brass doorknobs, light fixtures, and bathroom faucets that were being replaced. The soldiers took their treasures to the chaplain.

All together over 260 pounds of scrap brass was gathered. Captain Poch had a friend who had molds, and General Marshall had a friend in the right business to use them. The friend at the Oregon Brass Works of Portland agreed to take the old brass, melt it down, pour it into the molds and change all that old brass into two candlesticks and a cross, each weighing about forty pounds.

When the ornaments were delivered, they were full of impurities, which caused roughness, sharp edges, and tiny holes in the metal. They were different sizes, and rather dark, but they *were* real brass. Volunteers around the Barracks spent about 400 hours of 'elbow grease' in rubbing and polishing the new-old ornaments. General Marshall put in twenty hours of brass-shining time, too! Everyone felt better with proper altar equipment for the chapel, especially the chaplain.

To help keep up the men's social spirits, Mrs. Marshall and the General often opened their home to the men of Vancouver Barracks, especially on weekends, and especially for men without families. They had a pool table, provided refreshments, and made space for the men to meet and relax. They had not planned to open their home to the world, but one day, without planning to, they did.

On Sunday, June 20, 1937, General Marshall was reading his morning newspaper and waiting for his breakfast. The headlines told of three Russian fliers who were attempting the first non-stop flight from Moscow to San Francisco. While reading about the plane, he was told that the Russian plane was circling overhead and preparing to land on Pearson Air Field, very close to Vancouver Barracks. Practically in his front yard!

Bad weather and poor visibility had caused a change in the Russian plan. They could not make it to California, after all. Marshall ordered breakfast to be held, and for the cook to increase the number of servings. And off he hurried to meet the plane.

Around 8:30 he returned with the three men, Valerie P. Chkalov, Georgi P. Baidukov, and Alexander V. Beliakov. They were dirty and exhausted from the record-breaking, nonstop flight of 63 hours and 17 minutes. Marshall saw to it that they had baths, breakfast,

and beds and in that order. In fact, the men had part of their breakfast while soaking in their baths!

General Marshall told the local reporters and photographers,
who had quickly gathered outside the house, that the Russians
would not be talking, or available for pictures, until they had slept.
Soldiers were placed on guard at the foot of the staircase and in
front of the bedroom doors. But, the news was out!

The plane was truly a marvel to behold. It was a ANT-25 all
metal monoplane, with a wing span of 111 feet, six inches with a
single 950 horsepower engine. Built as a 10-passenger transport, it
had been turned into a flying gasoline tank in order to carry enough
fuel for the 5,228-mile flight. The Russians' accomplishment was a
marvel, also, and a milestone in aviation history, just as Charles
Lindbergh's flight from New York to Paris had been ten years
earlier.

Airplanes, and their advancing development, was of great interest to George C. Marshall. He was at Fort Leavenworth when he
first heard of Orville and Wilbur Wright and their first historic
flight. During the years since the Wright Brothers first flew at Kitty
Hawk, North Carolina, in 1903, the development of airplanes had
grown steadily. The world was becoming aware of the potential of
air power.

Radio announcers across the country were excitedly telling the
news. Marshall called the Soviet Ambassador, Alexander A.
Troyanovsky, to come from Oakland, California where he had been
waiting to congratulate his country's heroes. A planeload of national reporters came from Oakland where they had been waiting to
interview the men. The Russian leader, Joseph Stalin, and President
Franklin D. Roosevelt sent telegrams of congratulations to the
pilots.

While the heroes slept, General Marshall made preparations.
His study became a newsroom, and the living room was turned into
a press-conference room, both ready with several telephones for
radio broadcasts. Mrs. Marshall stepped in with a contribution to
the confusion and won everyone's approval when she brought out
a ham, bread and a G.I.-sized pot of coffee. The reporters remembered to thank her later in their articles that went out across the

General Marshall visiting with the Russian pilots and the Russian ambassador in his home at Vancouver Barracks in June 1937.

country by newspaper and radio. Everyone ate and waited for the men to finish sleeping.

In the meantime, George C. Marshall called Julius Meier, owner of the Meier and Frank Department Store, and arranged for an army truck to go to Portland. The truck brought back twenty suits and twenty sets of underwear, shirts, ties, belts, and shoes for the men. Tailors were sent to the rooms to help with the fittings, and the post barber was set up in a nearby room. A worldwide radio conference was broadcast that evening from the home of General and Mrs. George C. Marshall.

The landing of the Russians and all the publicity that followed was George C. Marshall's introduction to the nation, as well as theirs. He had no idea such an event would occur, yet he knew the right way to handle the situation in the best interests of his country. He reacted quickly and properly, with competence and diplomacy. He balanced the demands of the press and the public with his own ideas of hospitality so calmly and easily that he impressed everyone. Army officials in Washington, D.C. were especially pleased, and sent him commendations.

Marshall's name rose closer to the top of the Army's list of those marked for future advancement. The War Department generals were reminded, too, that airplanes could now cross the oceans, bringing the USA a little closer to the rest of the world.

Even with the excitement of foreign visitors, not all of Marshall's time was spent on Vancouver Barracks business. From the time of his arrival in the area, George C. Marshall spent a large part of his time directing Civilian Conservation Corps operations in his assigned district. Started nationally in 1933, the CCC men of the Pacific Northwest camps had accomplished a great deal of park, road, and bridge building by the time he arrived. Marshall was concerned for the construction and resource conservation of the area, but he was also concerned with the building of healthy minds and bodies. There were about 15,000 men and boys in the Vancouver CCC district.

Keeping healthy bodies for that many men, meant keeping many medical and dental records. According to Katherine Marshall's book, General Marshall talked a young army dentist, Lieutenant Edgar Alonzo Waterman, into doing a survey of the

TIME, May 2, 1938

FIRST LIEUT. E. A. WATERMAN
DENT-RES.
District Dental Officer

U. S. Teeth

After peering and prying into hundreds of Civilian Conservation Corps mouths, Dentist Edgar Alonzo Waterman of Portland, Ore. last week opened his own and spoke a large mouthful. Said Dentist Waterman: The best U. S. teeth come from Arkansas and Tennessee, the worst from New Jersey, New York and New England.

The explanation, according to Lieutenant Waterman: Southerners are in no hurry, take time to chew; the hard water of Arkansas' Ozark Mountains and of Tennessee's Cumberland Range contains minerals which help to build strong teeth. Easterners are always on the go, gulp and gobble their relatively soft food and water, lack exercise and fresh air.

• • •

CCC boys to find out which areas of the country produced the best and the worst teeth. The Pacific Northwest CCC camps had young men from many states all across America. Marshall's convincing point for the dentist was that never again would he have as many subjects, from so many states, in one place for such a survey. To everyone's surprise, especially the dentist's, the survey became somewhat famous. It was published locally, in the *Oregon Journal*, then in several dentistry journals, and finally, a short article appeared in *Time* magazine.

Just as with his first CCC camps in the South, Marshall believed in providing the boys with educational opportunities that would help them learn a trade. The Army provided tutors if any of them needed to learn reading, writing, and arithmetic. Marshall also believed the men should learn hobbies, sports, and recreational interests. He was always concerned with keeping the morale of the CCC men high. He encouraged them to do their best whether in their work, studies, or recreational lives.

One way to keep morale high was to praise and reward those who did well. Marshall kept track of who did what, when, and where in the CCC, and often mailed out personal letters of recognition citing accomplishments. If one did their assigned job well or did more than expected, they might receive a letter from General Marshall, and maybe a promotion to another, higher level, job. These letters were greatly appreciated and often useful as recommendations when the men applied for work after leaving the CCC.

Another way Marshall helped the men of the CCC was in starting a district newspaper, *The Review*. The paper came out twice a month with news of CCC activities, stories of personal and human interest, gossip, reports from every camp and no advertising. A six months individual subscription cost thirty-five cents. *The Review* was a connection between the men of the camps, it gave them identity and importance while secretly helping them with their reading and writing skills. Some of the CCC men who edited or wrote for the paper went on to have careers in newspaper work.

Following Marshall's suggestion, ten outstanding men were chosen from the thirty-five camps and given a trip to Portland. There, they were dinner guests at a Chamber of Commerce meeting where they each told their personal story. They described where

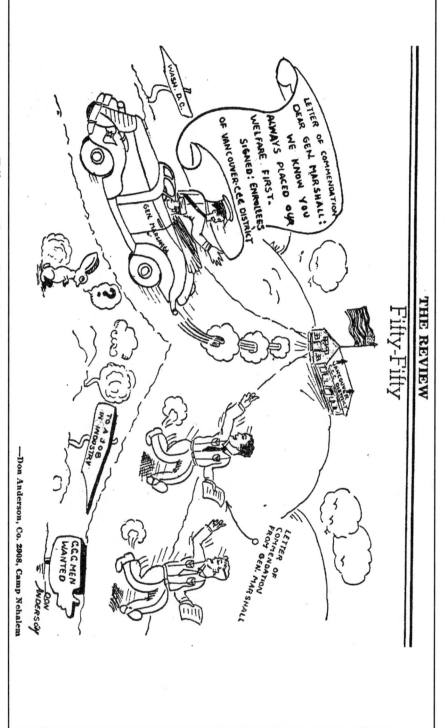

Tribute to General Marshall from *The Review*, the CCC newspaper

General and Mrs. Marshall on a fishing trip -- 1937

they came from, what the CCC had done for them, and what they hoped to do with their training in the future. The businessmen of the Portland area were impressed. They no longer thought of the CCC camps as just "work camps" after they learned how much good the CCC program was doing for those ten, as well as for the other thousands of men around the country.

As district commander, George C. Marshall enforced strict standards of cleanliness, orderliness and sanitation for his camps. His frequent and sometimes surprise visits to the CCC camps kept the camp directors on their guard and helped make sure the standards were met. But with twenty-five camps, throughout southern Washington and northern Oregon, and some of the camps were far apart, Marshall's inspection responsibilities were huge. He needed help.

He appointed three sub-district commanders, Captain Jack W. Kittrell, Captain V.J. Gregory, and Captain Alfred H. Hopkins to help him make the inspection visits. They checked on the camp directors and reported any problems or needs to General Marshall.

Having assistants did not mean that Marshall did not go on inspection tours himself. Frequently, he took Mrs. Marshall along with him. The scenery of the great Northwest was worth the trip for them both, it also gave the Marshalls some private time away from the military base and Vancouver activity. They spent the weekends at wooded cabins or small hotels along the way, as they went from camp to camp.

Katherine Marshall wrote, "We spent many days together in that magnificent country on inspection trips. Without a driver, but always with a cooking outfit in the back of the car, we would be down in the valleys. . . .and the next hour we would be high up in snow-covered mountains with great canyons at our sides; then down in again through the lava beds."

Sometimes the Marshalls invited the General's adjutant, Major Claude M. (Flap) Adams, and his wife for a weekend in the northwest country. Major Adams had a sense of humor that appealed to General Marshall, and he was not afraid to use it. They both enjoyed playing practical jokes, ones that were funny. Often they joined forces to play jokes on others, but sometimes worked even harder to trick each other.

Once, during an awards ceremony at Vancouver Barracks, General Marshall called Flap Adams to come forward, said some very nice things about him, and presented him with a gift. In the box was a watch. Adams was surprised and even impressed to be so recognized. He thanked General Marshall, took the watch, and went back to his seat. Mrs. Marshall whispered to him that perhaps he, "should look carefully at that watch." When he did, Major Adams discovered that it was his own watch he had received as a gift. George C. Marshall had struck again!

In the summer of 1938, General Marshall received new orders. He was called back to Washington and to the War Department by General Malin Craig, Chief of Staff of the Army, who needed Marshall's help in the War Plans Division. After a few weeks of farewell fishing, and saying good-byes to their friends, the Marshalls were packed and ready to go. Many parties and special dinners were given in his honor, both on post and in the community. On the evening before they left, the Vancouver High School and the 7th Infantry bands came to the Marshalls' house to serenade them.

General and Mrs. Marshall were greatly missed at Vancouver Barracks, in the community, and in the CCC camps when their great Northwest adventure was finished. In sadness at leaving a favorite place, yet with excitement at the idea of a new assignment, they headed East by train. Mrs. Marshall and Molly went to their home on Fire Island, New York, for a vacation, but George C. Marshall went to work at the War Department.

Reporting for Duty

Chapter 12

Generally Speaking

July 1938 – December 1941

George C. Marshall sweltered along with everyone else. In the eleven years he had lived away from the nation's capital, he had forgotten how hot and humid the city's summer could be. He might rather be fishing for salmon in Washington State, but he dutifully went to his office in Washington, D.C., on July 7, 1938, among the cars and the noise, the government buildings, and the other busy people. The Vancouver Barracks, the CCC, and the rustic beauty of the Pacific Northwest were far, far behind him. His new assignment, assistant chief of staff in the War Plans Division (WPD) of the General Staff in the War Department, kept him extremely busy, regardless of the weather.

While Mrs. Marshall and Molly vacationed at the beach, the General settled into his job and looked for a house. The Marshalls were expected to live near his work, but they wanted to live in the country, outside the city. For one reason or another, he found no house that suited him. He finally leased a house at 2118 Wyoming Avenue, just off of Connecticut Avenue, not far from Rock Creek Park, and decided it would have to do.

The house did just fine. Katherine Marshall was content to live near the edge of the city. Having a house with trees around it, and not living on a regular Army post gave them some added privacy. They were Army folks, after all, and would adjust themselves, from the country to the city. At least, they were close enough to his office so that he could walk to work.

During those first months in Washington, Marshall was so busy he had no time for his regular exercise routines, particularly the walking and horseback riding, which he had enjoyed in Vancouver. Katherine helped him work out a scheme that was good for both of them. He walked the two miles to his office in the Old Post Office Building in the morning. After work, he called her before he left the office, she met him half way, and they walked home together. In that way, they could talk and catch up on their day's happenings and their exercise at the same time.

The news from Europe and Asia was disturbing, and Marshall's job in the War Department quickly had him involved in tension-filled discussions of national security. He helped make decisions regarding the war-like actions of Nazi Germany, fascist Italy, and militarist Japan. One thing General Marshall knew for sure: if another Great War was coming, the United States should not wait too long to prepare its defenses.

Three months later, in October, Marshall was promoted to deputy chief of staff of the Army. General Malin Craig was his boss, and Craig, who was the Army chief of staff, was planning to retire within a year. A younger general would be appointed by President Roosevelt to take his place, and Marshall had hopes of being the one. Meanwhile, as deputy chief of staff, he had significant influence in getting America's army ready for the war, the war he feared was sure to come.

He spent many hours in meetings discussing the trouble in Europe and what the United States should do for self-protection, while still not in the war. On November 14, 1938, President Roosevelt called a White House Conference of selected men, including George C. Marshall, to discuss some urgent issues of possible war preparation. The President had a new plan and he outlined it to the group. He planned to ask Congress for funds to build 10,000 airplanes per year. He proposed selling most of the planes to England and France. In that way, they could be used for fighting, Germany might be defeated, but the U.S. could basically stay out of the war.

To Marshall, the plan seemed unbalanced and made little, if any, military sense. Without pilots, support crew, and ground forces, he saw no advantage to American defense in it. No one else at the

General Marshall carries his old battered briefcase, one of his prized possessions since World War I , October 11, 1940. (Harris & Ewing photo)

meeting seemed to disagree with President Roosevelt. Asking around the group for approval, after explaining his plan, the President finally asked General Marshall, "Don't you think so, George?" Marshall did not.

George C. Marshall was not afraid to speak out, and he did not like the President's use of his first name. No one called General Marshall 'George' except his family and his close friends, and the President was neither of those. Everyone in the room, especially President Roosevelt, was surprised when Marshall answered, "I'm sorry, Mr. President, but I don't agree with that at all."

Like General John Pershing, when confronted with Marshall in 1917, the President appeared a bit surprised, and he adjourned the meeting quickly. As in 1917, the others who heard Marshall's answer began telling him good-bye. They figured his brief stay as deputy chief of staff was over. Still, as Wendy Lubetkin wrote, "Roosevelt appeared startled, but like Pershing years earlier, he was not the sort of man who was offended by the truth."

Again, like Pershing, in the months that followed the November disagreement, the President often asked Marshall's advice concerning the U.S. military situation. Marshall was worried about the 1938-39 conditions of national defense. When the U.S. entered the first worldwide war, they had not been prepared, and he did not want to see his country repeat its mistakes of 1917. To him, it was the same old problem. He told Roosevelt the nation's army and air forces were completely unready for war. Marshall was honest, accurate, and definite in his assessment.

In 1939, the U.S. Army ranked 17th in the world; even Bulgaria and Portugal had larger armies. At that time, an army field division was a unit of infantry (foot soldiers) of about seventeen or eighteen thousand men with rifles, machine guns, small and large cannons. Germany had 90 field divisions, Italy had forty-five, and Japan had fifty on the Chinese mainland. The United States Army, which included the Air Corps, had only nine divisions (on paper) and none were completely ready to fight at wartime strength. The Army and Army Air Corps together had about 165,000 officers and enlisted men. Marshall knew the facts and he was worried.

The retiring Chief of Staff, General Malin Craig, welcomes his successor General George C. Marshall to the job at the War Department, June 28, 1939.   (Harris and Ewing photo)

As deputy chief of staff, it was Marshall's business to be concerned. He was only one step away from becoming the top-notch officer in the U.S. Army. He was determined to increase the size and strength of the army, and sometimes he disagreed with President Roosevelt, the Commander in Chief of all the armed forces, on what should be done first. Would that not hurt his chances for becoming Roosevelt's choice for the Army's new chief of staff?

It has been said that Roosevelt reached past thirty some generals to select George C. Marshall as chief of staff. That is partly true. Recent Army rules required a general to be young enough to serve a four year term before he reached the age of sixty-four. Seniority was still the rule of Army promotion in 1938-39, but several factors were in Marshall's favor. One was his age. Of the thirty-three generals ahead of Marshall on the seniority list, twenty-nine could not qualify in age. That moved Marshall into fifth place.

Of the other four generals in the running, none had a record quite as impressive as Marshall's. Marshall also knew he had three men on his side. General Craig, General John Pershing, and one of Roosevelt's cabinet members and friends, Harry Hopkins, all favored Marshall. Both Pershing and Hopkins made their wishes known to FDR, but Roosevelt alone would make the choice. All Marshall could do was wait.

Marshall did not take it for granted that he would be chosen for the top spot, but he did nothing to influence the President's decision, either. George C. Marshall was not a politician. While Roosevelt made up his mind, Marshall simply continued to concentrate his energies on plans for improving and rebuilding the national defense.

On Sunday, April 23, 1939, the president summoned Marshall to the White House. It seems no other War Department members were present when Franklin D. Roosevelt told George C. Marshall that, beginning September first, he would succeed General Malin Craig as chief of staff of the Army. Marshall was pleased, but still had some concern.

General Marshall said, "I saw the President in his study when he told me. It was an interesting interview. I told him I wanted the right to say what I think and it would often be unpleasing. I said,

'Is that all right?' He (Roosevelt) said, 'Yes.' I said, 'You said yes pleasantly, but it may be unpleasant.' "

Marshall left the President's office still a bit unsure the job was really his. But Roosevelt had decided; he was sure. He knew Marshall might be short in his words, but he was long on the truth. Years later, another president, Harry S. Truman said, "A man either tells the truth or he doesn't. General Marshall was the exemplification of the man of truth." General Marshall knew, on that April Sunday, the truth must soon be told to the American public. War was coming. His appointment as chief of staff was announced on April 27, 1939.

In May, the U.S. Army Chief of Staff was invited to visit Brazil, in a diplomatic effort to help guard against German and Italian military influences becoming stronger there. Since General Craig would soon leave office, he decided to send General Marshall in his place. Marshall was quickly and seriously learning about international diplomacy, national politics, and global armed forces. He and his staff made the Brazil trip a good-will trip, successfully impressed the Brazilian government, and helped secure the safety of the Western Hemisphere.

According to Katherine Marshall's writings, the Brazilian Military Band that met General Marshall only knew one U.S. military tune to play and, "they struck up that tune when General Marshall stepped off the ship and whenever he appeared in public thereafter. He had a hard time keeping his face straight . . ." whenever Anchors Aweigh, the Navy's song, was played for him. He must have thought about the words of the last line, 'Sink the Army, sink the Army gray' while standing at attention so far away from an Army-Navy football game, and his home.

Back home in Washington, General Craig took his last two months of vacation time and left the office on July 1, 1939. Marshall became, in all respects, the real chief of staff of the army. All of the responsibilities and duties of the job fell from Malin Craig's shoulders onto George C. Marshall 's that day. Officially, Marshall's title would not change for another two months. He was still the "acting chief of staff," and he acted, all right, but he certainly was not "acting."

114

September 1, 1939, General George C. Marshall was sworn in as Chief of
Staff of the U.S. Army by Major General Emory Adams.

On the night of August 31, 1939 the Marshalls had dinner with friends and looked forward with excitement to the next day. A swearing in ceremony and a reception were scheduled to celebrate General Marshall becoming the new chief of staff of the army.

The evening was pleasant, except for a dinner time phone call that alerted General Marshall to possible worries in the making. He did not elaborate, or leave the dinner party, and the rest of the evening passed quietly.

Seldom does one receive good news by telephone in the middle of the night. Forrest C. Pogue began the first volume of his Marshall biographies with this powerful sentence: "At three o'clock in the morning of September 1, 1939, General George C. Marshall, acting Chief of Staff of the United States Army, was wakened by the telephone." The bad news had come.

It was not unexpected news. Adolph Hitler's armies had crossed the borders of Poland, and German planes were bombing Warsaw. Since England and France had sworn to defend Poland against German aggression, they must begin to fight back. World War II had begun. General Marshall went to his office immediately, in the middle of the night.

The special ceremony planned for Marshall's inauguration was canceled, and instead he was sworn in quickly and quietly by The Adjutant General in the office of the secretary of war, just before noon on September 1, 1939. In between that early morning phone call and being sworn in, Marshall received the fastest promotions of his life. He was promoted to the permanent rank of major general, and at the same time, to the temporary rank of General, U.S. Regular Army, as he finally replaced General Malin Craig. His borrowed job was over; the new one belonged to him.

As the highest ranking officer in the U.S. Army, Marshall wore four stars on his uniform. It probably surprised him to think he had advanced from one star to four, when only three years before he had no stars! At age fifty-nine, he had reached the top of his chosen profession. He was the commander of all the other army generals, and would be responsible for making many serious decisions. You might say he was president of the U.S. Army.

Marshall soon wrote to Malin Craig, "My day of induction into office was momentous, with the starting of what appears to be a

World War...You know, I think you timed your affairs very beautifully because you certainly left me on a hot spot."

It surely was a hot spot. When the European and Asian wars became World War II, and before the U.S. entered the war, Marshall began to push for increased funding for the U.S. Army. Everything required more money, and Congress controlled the funding. President Roosevelt wanted to enlarge the Navy and the Air Corps, and General Marshall wanted more Infantry troops, artillery, and equipment, as well as airplanes for the Air Corps.

On September 8, 1939, the President issued his "Limited Emergency Proclamation" which authorized the expansion of the active army and the National Guard. The War Department was directed to purchase $12 million dollars worth of motor transportation. Marshall knew that amount would not be enough, but it was a beginning. George C. Marshall was encouraged.

On September 8, also, General and Mrs. Marshall went to visit his hometown in Pennsylvania. He had been invited to Uniontown several months before, for the celebration of "Marshall Day." Ten thousand people were at the airport to greet him, including his sister, Marie. Speeches were made and receptions were held in the homecoming celebration for him.

A local newspaper ran a long article honoring him, and this is part of it: "For almost 40 years, General Marshall, you have been preparing for the position you now hold, for the great burden for which you are now responsible, and to you, as Chief of Staff of the United States Army, our special welcome is for "Flicker," the snub-nosed, freckle-faced red-head who was a natural-born leader of boydom in the 90's, who coasted on Gilmore's Hill, staged shows in Thompson's stable, and kept things generally astir. Today we hope you can lay aside your honors and your burdens and make friends with your youth. Flicker Marshall has been gone for such a long, long time."

In the evening, after visiting several scenes of his youth around town, he spoke at a dinner, in The White Swan Hotel which was built on the site of the old tavern he had known of as a boy. Four hundred guests listened to him talk of the French and Indian War, George Washington, General Braddock, and the historical importance of the entire Uniontown area. He connected the importance of those past times to the present. He said that Americans should daily be thankful to live where they do, think as they do, and are able to enjoy blessings that could become rare privileges on this earth. The new chief of staff spoke new words to remember in his old hometown.

Along with being chief of staff, came another change in the Marshalls' housing. In late September of 1939, they moved into Quarters I at Fort Myer, which was where they would live for the next six years. Within the next year, Katherine Marshall tried to make the house a get-away place, a place for some peace and quiet. General Marshall needed to rest sometimes, to relax and not think of war and weapons, money and machines, supplies and soldiers. He needed a place to gather strength for fighting the next day's office battle, and forget the world for a few hours.

Quarters 1 worked well for them. It was a large brick house with an upstairs sun porch where they could relax, read and talk, or have their meals. Quarters 1 was close enough to his office that he could come home for lunch and a short nap. His secretary called the house when he left the office, and his lunch was on the table when he arrived. Sometimes he brought friends or staff members with him. It puzzled his guests that somehow lunch was ready for them, too.

He was an excellent staff officer, and did some of his best planning within a group. Rather than making statements of his own opinion, he would steer the discussions, by asking important questions that would lead the group to the conclusion he wanted. According to Forrest C. Pogue, "By inheritance, by training, and by prolonged work with civilians, he was aware of the strength and the weaknesses of democratic government, and he was wholly prepared to fit his role to that system."

Being chief of staff was never an easy job. The situation is different for each chief of staff. Some people complained that Marshall was not trained in formal ideas and philosophy, military science, or international economics. Yet, a person could not take classes or have a classic formal training for being chief of staff. There was no set formula or pattern to follow. Marshall had natural talents and know-how. Marshall was a man with tremendous determination, and a strong capacity to learn. He was a master of self-discipline,

Home of the Army's Chief of Staff -- Quarters I at Fort Myer, Virginia

knowledge of his subject, professionalism, and sincerity. He usually knew instinctively what to do. If he did not know, he found someone who did.

As he fitted himself into his job, people became aware of his honesty and loyalty. They learned to trust what he said and to believe in what he did.

Marshall's influence with Congress grew immensely during 1940. His experiences with legislators, from his days of working with General Pershing in 1920-24, and his days with the Illinois National Guard during the 1930s, proved useful at this time. He understood, more than most people, the duties of a soldier in a democracy. He believed in the citizen soldier. He and his staff often appeared at hearings and gatherings in civilian clothes rather than uniforms. Marshall thought that might help assure the people that he worked for them, he just happened to work for them through the Army.

Now and then, he used stories from his childhood to ease the tension in the Congress. In one of his first appearances before a congressional committee the chairman said, "'I imagine that you are not accustomed to dealing with members of the Congress." The General said that he had some knowledge of Congress.

He told them that as a boy in Pennsylvania he and a friend had once written to their representative for their advertised "free seeds" to plant in their greenhouse. The seeds arrived, and they were amazed to find that the packages contained cotton seeds. The boys were not sure that cotton would grow in Pennsylvania. All the same, they planted them, trusting in the superior knowledge of the Washington legislators about seeds. They were disappointed when the plants produced no cotton. But then, it was Pennsylvania, and cotton does not grow there. He finished his story with, "So you see, I have been knowing about Congress for a long time. "

Even when poking a little fun at the Congressmen, he was absolutely serious about building the national defense through the army. With any congressional investigating committee, Marshall was always respectful, patient, and cooperative. His statements and answers were factual, accurate and in the interest of the entire nation, not just Republicans or Democrats. He usually spoke without notes in congressional hearings. He had an impressive ability to memorize a vast amount of information and to bring it out when he needed it.

Beginning in the summer of 1939 and on into the autumn of 1941, he appeared forty-eight times before various House and Senate committees to talk of the necessary needs of the country's armed forces. He was not an accomplished speaker, especially when reading a speech, but he could overwhelm an audience with his knowledge of facts and his passionate belief in what he was saying, when he spoke without notes.

Congressmen might disagree with Marshall, and they might question and argue, but they knew he was telling them the truth. Speaker of the House of Representatives, Sam Rayburn said, "He has the presence of a great man. He would tell the truth even if it hurt his own cause (the Army)." Congress always respected him and would give him things they would give no one else."

Forrest C. Pogue wrote, "That respect grew when Marshall rejected additional funds that he had not asked for and said they were emotional "enthusiasms" that could not be allowed to interfere with rational planning. The "flag-waving days of warfare are gone," he told Congress. "I have but one purpose, one mission, and that is to produce the most efficient Army in the world."

In February of 1940, Marshall told one congressional committee, "If Europe blazes in the late spring or early summer, we must put our house in order before the sparks reach the Western Hemisphere."

As with Congress, Marshall's influence with the President grew in 1940. Beginning with the day that Marshall first disagreed with Roosevelt, they had numerous conferences and conflicts. In accepting his position as chief of staff, Marshall had warned the President that he would not always be agreeable to the President's ideas and he reserved the right to disagree.

By the winter of 1944, Marshall was Roosevelt's primary advisor concerning the war. Marshall came to appreciate the President's special style of governing, but he did not go to his parties or dinners or socialize easily with the President; he would not even laugh at the President's jokes. Roosevelt and Marshall were never close friends, but they respected each other and appreciated the responsibilities of their specific positions.

One example of Marshall's persuasive technique with President Roosevelt occurred in the spring of 1940. Marshall was taken by Secretary of Treasury Henry Morgenthau to see the President, asking for backing to approach Congress for more war department money. FDR was not ready to give his approval, and evaded dealing with their request.

Fearing they would have to leave without convincing him of the need, Marshall stepped over to the President's chair and asked quietly, but intently, " Mr. President, may I have three minutes?" The President agreed to listen, even when Marshall took longer than three minutes. With his voice full of frustration, anger, and concern, Marshall laid out the list of defense needs for the Army and the country, finishing with, "If you don't do something, and do it right away, I don't know what is going to happen to this country." Morgenthau later wrote in his diary about Marshall, "He stood right up to the President."

But Roosevelt's answer was cold, and short, without his usual friendly bantering, "Thank you, General. And thank you, Henry," was all he said. Marshall and Morgenthau gathered up their papers to leave. As they reached the door, the President said, "Oh General, come back and see me tomorrow. And bring me a list in detail of your requirements." That, according to General Marshall, was a turning point for the defense budget.

Two weeks later the President asked Congress for a defense budget of $1 billion dollars. In one of his radio speeches Marshall told the American people, "For the first time in our history, we are beginning to prepare against the possibility of war. For almost twenty years we had all the time and no money, today we have all the money and no time,"

In the spring of 1940, Katherine Marshall began to look for a house to buy out in the country, away from Fort Myer. She wrote, "Whenever I could find time I would drive through the Virginia countryside to look for a place near Washington where we could spend weekends when summer came . . . that spring (1940) we bought "Dodona Manor" in Leesburg. Although only 35 miles from Washington, the place had been ours for months before General Marshall had a chance to see it." He did not have time for house hunting, and left the job up to her.

General Marshall talks with Secretary of War Henry Stimson.

He was too busy building his army. In the spring of 1940, the first peacetime draft in American history was proposed. General Marshall said, "I believe that Selective Service provides the only practical and economical method of maintaining the military forces that we inevitably are going to be required to have in the future and I think with all of my heart that Selective Service is a necessity to the maintenance of a true democracy."

In August of 1940, President Roosevelt signed the Selective Service Act and authorized the National Guard to be called into service. By September of 1940, Congress had agreed to the appropriations, the draft, and to calling up the Reserves as well as the National Guard, which enabled the army to grow to 800,000 by December. The newspaper headlines read: "Marshall Urges U.S. to Prepare" and "New Boss—New Army."

Finding enough living spaces and enough equipment for the growing number of soldiers was a headache all its own. Basic requirements of clothing, housing, hospitals, and training grounds for troops were uppermost on the mind of the chief of staff. Slowly, the new, updated Army began to take shape. It took hard work, many people, a lot of money, and more than a year, but George C. Marshall changed the U.S. Army into the largest and most powerful in the world. His schedule was full and he was constantly on the phone, writing letters, assigning jobs, or traveling.

"During this expansion of the Army, so many thousands of new ideas and inventions were sent to the War Department that it was difficult to separate the wheat from the chaff." Marshall expected his staff to do the separating, but if they found a new and practical idea, they were to pass it on for his approval or disapproval. He was always looking for ways to improve the efficiency of the Army.

"His immediate staff had access to his office at all times but there was nothing that annoyed him more than to have one of them open the door, look in, and seeing he was busy, back out . . .he had a notice put on his office door: 'Once you open this door, WALK IN, no matter what is going on inside' . . . One day Colonel Bedell Smith, Secretary of the General Staff, opened the door ... and he almost backed out when he saw several generals in conference. General Marshall said, "Come in, Smith. Didn't you see that sign?

The original Willys-Overland pilot model delivered to the U.S. Army on November 11, 1940.

Now what is it?" Colonel Smith explained there was a man in his office whom he would like General Marshall to see."

The man in question represented the Bantam Car Company of Butler, Pennsylvania and had brought to Washington drawings of a small, sturdy car which he wished to offer the Government for a test. He had been sent from one person to another, one department to another, and finally ended up in Marshall's office. He was very discouraged, and figured it was his last stop. Nobody seemed interested. Colonel Smith thought the car plans looked promising, and suggested that Marshall should talk with him.

Instead, Marshall asked Smith had he gone over the plans, and what did he think. Smith said that he thought the idea was a "find", and Marshall said to order one. Smith said they should order fifteen to do a real test. Marshall asked how much that would cost and when he heard $12,000 he asked if Smith could find the money in the budget, and when he replied that he could, Marshall said, "Very well. Do it." And that was how the Army found their first Jeep.

The General Purpose Vehicle, (G.P.) was later called a Jeep. Another origin of the name came from a little character, Eugene the Jeep, in the newspaper comic strip *Popeye*, who had special powers and could do almost anything. So could that small-size, truck-car! The Armored Forces had turned down the plan, but three weeks after the Army accepted the plan, they ordered 39,000. After testing and revisions, Ford Motor Company, and Willys-Overland had manufactured about 650,000 by the end of the war. George C. Marshall called the Jeep, "this country's most important contribution to the war." If only all of his problems had been as easy to settle as deciding on the jeep!

Marshall set himself a new and rigid schedule. He was up before 6:30 and in his office by 7:30. At noon he went back to for lunch with Katherine, followed by a ten or fifteen minute nap, returning to his office at one o'clock to work until five. Marshall said that "no one had an original thought after 3 p.m." and thought all work should be left at the office. He did not avoid hard and steady work, and he liked to be organized. Being organized and sticking to a strict routine, helped him maintain his physical and mental health. When he left work, he left a clean desktop behind him and would, "completely detach myself from Army affairs."

Marshall's doctor warned him about gaining weight, so early in the morning or late in the afternoon he went horseback riding to help keep down his "desk belly." Sometimes he rode with Molly, his stepdaughter, and sometimes with Rose Page, his goddaughter. Other days he went swimming in the Fort Myer pool. Evenings were often spent in required social activities, but more often taking a walk with Katherine, or canoeing on the Potomac River. They sometimes went to the post movie theater for one of his favorite escapes, a good old-fashioned western. Always he tried to be in bed by 9 p.m.

Even when he exercised and seemed to relax, Mrs. Marshall was concerned that the General had no time for himself. He had not had a real vacation in a long time. At her urging, they planned a trip in October of 1940 to see a VMI football game. It had been a hot summer with no time off and pressure every day. He was not sleeping well at night and Mrs. Marshall thought he needed a break. As luck would have it, the Secretary of War Henry Stimson and his wife announced a formal reception for the General Staff for the same Saturday the Marshalls planned to be away.

George C. Marshall felt they should attend the reception, but Katherine thought differently. She told Secretary Stimson of her concern. Stimson agreed, and asked her how he could persuade Marshall to forget the reception. She said, "By direct order. That is the only way." The next morning a written order from the President, and signed by Stimson, was handed to General Marshall in his office. He was directed to attend the VMI - Davidson football game over the weekend. "During said period he shall be under the exclusive control and direction of Mrs. Marshall and shall be protected against all interruptions, particularly by members of the War Department and of the Congress." The Marshalls saw VMI win that game by a score of 13-7.

Mark Stoler wrote, "By late 1940, even Marshall's daily schedule had to be modified under the increasing pressures of work. Marshall gave up entertaining, accepting invitations, maintaining old contacts and friendships, or answering the telephone at night." The Marshalls avoided the social scene of Washington as much as possible and he ducked personal publicity as much as he could.

General Marshall talks to men of the Army Air Corps,
Fort Benning, Georgia -- 1941.

He made an exception to social calls with his scheduled visits to the aging General John J. Pershing in Walter Reed Hospital. Pershing was delighted with Marshall's appointment to chief of staff, and Marshall felt he should keep him informed of the action, even when General Pershing sometimes found it hard to remember the details of their conversations.

In August of 1941, Marshall began planning the Army's strategy, in case war came to the United States. He brought home maps at night and talked out his plans, although Katherine had trouble following him as she listened. She said that some evenings it would be the Pacific, another night Europe, Africa, or the Panama Canal. She wondered how he would ever remember all the places involved. All she knew to do was pray that he would be given enough time to get his army ready before it was needed.

During the fall of 1941, General Marshall went out on inspection trips, learning what the soldiers needed, and watching maneuvers at army and air bases around the country. The main reason to watch maneuvers was to watch the generals and the colonels. It was on the training fields of Texas, Louisiana, North Carolina, and other places that he first saw Omar Bradley, Dwight Eisenhower, and George Patton in action.

Marshall was keenly interested in the progress of troop training and wanted to see for himself the results of his orders to commanding officers. He often chatted with soldiers to see if they had questions or complaints. If there was anything they needed and did not have, he made sure someone knew about it as soon as possible. Preparing the soldiers and air corps for the war he knew would soon involve the United States was his main concern.

In late November of 1941, General Marshall and the other chiefs of staff knew that something big concerning Japan was likely to happen. They just did not know for certain when or exactly where it would be. He thought the Japanese might attack the Philippine Islands, because they were in the way of Japan's drive Southward. He warned General MacArthur to keep his troops on guard. Many meetings with President Roosevelt and Secretary of State Cordell Hull occurred without any firm answers or actions.

On the morning of December 7, 1941 George C. Marshall had breakfast with Katherine and then went for his regular Sunday morning horseback ride. Just as he returned, the phone rang. The message was urgent. He quickly changed clothes and left for his office.

Intercepted Japanese diplomatic codes had warned Washington that Japan was breaking off relations with the United States as of 1:00 p.m. that day. By noon, telegrams were written and sent in code by radio to the four key commanders in the Pacific telling them to be on the alert. The message to Hawaii was delayed by transmission difficulties and was not delivered until after the attack began at 7:50 a.m. Honolulu time —12:50 Washington D.C. time. The next message that came to Washington was AIR RAID — AIR RAID ON PEARL HARBOR ——— THIS IS NOT A DRILL!

According to Lubetkin, "The series of errors and misunderstandings that led to the destruction of the American fleet at Pearl Harbor would be almost comic had the result not been the loss of 2,403 American lives, 6 battleships, and 180 planes."

Japan had bombed Pearl Harbor. America was going to war.

George C. Marshall talks with President Roosevelt at the
Casablanca Conference in 1943.

Reporting for Duty

Chapter 13

Washington Daze

December 7, 1941 —— June 6,1944

The news of the attack at Pearl Harbor reached Washington shortly after 1 p.m. on Sunday. George C. Marshall did not go home until after seven that December evening. Katherine was waiting for him. She wrote, "When he came in, his face was grim and grey. What was in his mind, I do not know; but this I did know: Since June 1938—-three and a half years—he had labored relentlessly against impossible odds to arouse and prepare America . . . George said nothing except that he was tired and was going to bed."

The time of preparing for war was past. War had arrived. American armed forces must be mobilized and directed in the fighting of what would be called "*the big one*," the Second World War, and World War II. Never before had one war been fought in so many places at the same time over such large areas. The battlefield was the world. The problems of organizing troops, supplies, and war plans were unusual and difficult. George C. Marshall and his U.S. Army would be severely tested during the next months and years.

By December 8, 1941, the U.S. had declared war on Japan, and on December 12th also on Germany and Italy. As bad as Pearl Harbor was, some good may have come from it. It convinced the American public that the war was not only in Europe and Asia, but could be in their country, too. The threat of the airplane as a weapon of war became real.

In planning land battles, General Marshall was directing troops in both Europe and the Pacific, on six continents, and in two hemi-

General Marshall and staff discuss war plans in his office - 1941. L-R: Brig. Gen. Leonard T. Gerow, Brig. Gen. R.A. Wheeler, Brig. Gen. Sherman Miles, Maj. Gen. Henry H. Arnold, Gen. Marshall, Brig. Gen. W.H. Haislip, Brig. Gen. Harry L. Twaddle, Maj. Gen. William Bryden.

spheres. Marshall could not do everything; he needed able assistants. General H.H. (Hap) Arnold was in charge of the Army Air Corps. Hap Arnold, had been with Marshall in the Philippines in 1914, knew about airplanes and flying and the Air Corps was a vital part of the armed forces. He became Marshall's right hand man, and the two of them worked well together. If Arnold was his right hand, Secretary of War, Henry Stimson was Marshall's strong right arm. Stimson helped bridge the gap between government policy and the action of the army. Teamwork and cooperation between the War Department, Congress, the President, and America's allied nations was necessary. The free world was fighting for survival.

Because Germany was considered the greatest threat, the war against it would have to be won first, before the war against Japan could be won. Marshall's problems multiplied quickly in number and importance. His task was enormous and exhausting.

Marshall and his staff contacted business people whose factories could be changed from producing civilian clothing to making uniforms, from making regular shoes to making Army shoes and boots, and instead of cars, make tanks and army trucks. Ammunition plants were built and went to work making powder for bullets, hand grenades and bombs.

With the draft in effect, thousands of soldiers entered the Army every month. The army and air corps bases needed barracks, bedding, kitchens, food, uniforms, shoes, hospitals, medicine, —— the lists seemed endless. Troops, supplies, and equipment were needed in the Pacific. Guns, ships, tanks, and airplanes had to be manufactured faster and faster, not only for the American army but for all the Allied armies. Fast production and the shipment of troops and supplies to all parts of the world at the same time was necessary, but was terribly difficult. Which battle to fight first, which troops should get what and when, and which general should he send where?

By the spring of 1942, most of George and Katherine Marshall's family, of fighting age, was enlisted in the armed forces. Her two sons, Clifton and Allen, her brother and her niece and nephew were all in training and would see service overseas. Naturally, they were concerned for their own family, but Marshall was also concerned for all Army families.

Early in the war years, George C. Marshall wrote personal letters to families of men who were killed. He managed to keep up for awhile, but when the lists of deaths, those taken prisoner, or missing in action grew longer and longer, he simply could not write to everyone. He changed to sending a standard printed card, or note addressed by his secretaries, that he could simply sign. He received thousands of thank you notes and responses. George C. Marshall hated the personal and family losses that came with war.

The personal pain of war came to the Marshalls when Katherine's son, 2nd Lieutenant Allen Tupper Brown, a tank commander with the First Armored Division on assignment in Italy, was killed by a sniper's single bullet on May 29, 1944. Marshall was deeply saddened by the death of his favorite stepson. When he was in Italy, in June, not long after D-Day, General Marshall located and visited Allen's gravesite, one among 7,000 graves near Anzio beachhead. He wanted to be able to tell Katherine and Allen's wife that he had seen it. He then went to "identify the scene of Allen's last action," and, from a small airplane and using one of Allen's own crumpled maps, was able to pinpoint the exact spot where Allen had been when he was killed. Somehow, after seeing the scene and Allen's grave, understanding what had happened and talking to the men who had known Allen, Marshall was better able to accept the fact of Allen's death.

If he was concerned for anyone's welfare, General Marshall was concerned for his infantrymen, his G.I. Joes. All the enlisted men were known as G.I.s because their clothes from outside to inside, top to bottom were Government Issue, with the label sewn or painted on, so the nickname G.I. came to life. The name Joe was stuck on, perhaps because it was a common name, just like the issued items were common to everyone, thus the origin of G.I. Joe. George C. Marshall worked long and hard to make sure the G.I.s had what they needed when they needed it. Candy bars and cokes, even hot Thanksgiving turkey dinners were brought to the G.I. Joes in the foxholes on the front line of fire!

Marshall worked out one idea for increasing the soldiers' morale that paid off in a great way. He thought American troops, especially the infantry soldier, should know why the country was fighting a war. What was it the foot soldier was fighting for, why was he told to leave his home and family, to risk his life? Marshall felt the soldiers had a right to know, and he had a duty to tell them.

Movies and radio were the entertainment technologies of the time. George C. Marshall was fond of movies, especially western movies, so he decided that a movie about what had started the war, what they might expect to see in war, how war was being fought, etc. would help explain things. As he told Forrest C. Pogue, ". . . I called in Frank Capra, the leading motion picture director at that time, and had him prepare the films (*Why We Fight* – a set of 6 films) which were a complete education, I think, on the war . . . they are one of the best educational set-ups that I have ever seen, and they were interesting and they were done very expertly. They were amusing, — they were serious — they were tremendous in their scope. . . I was raising an army and I required that every soldier see that (series) before he left the United States. . ."

Frank Capra hesitated to commit to making the films. He had directed several regular movies with great success, but he told General Marshall that he had never made a documentary before, and Marshall replied, "Capra, I have never been Chief of Staff before." That did it. Capra combined newsreel films and army-made movies from actual fighting and bombing scenes from Britain, Europe and Asia into a series of six, hour-long films.

Marshall had the films made, as he said, . . . "on the Q.T. (quiet) I never allowed the secretary of war to see it, or the White House to see it until we had it finished." He was glad the media had been an answer to his problem on one side. On the other, with the press corps, it created somewhat of another problem.

George C. Marshall liked music as well as movies, and he made a small contribution to another form of entertainment. He had fun helping Irving Berlin, as Berlin wrote the music for a hit stage production called, "You're In the Army Now." Marshall knew that relaxation and entertainment was important for soldiers. He was on an inspection tour of a base in Georgia, and went into the nearest town, rented a room, dressed in civilian clothes, and took a walk around town. He wanted to know what the soldiers from the base did when they came into town on their daylong or weekend pass.

The town had a city park and wide streets, and several decent eating places, but he said, "The net result was . . . I never got anything to eat until half past ten....there wasn't a place to sit down. . . the town was so overstocked with soldiers that there wasn't anywhere that you could relax." He was worried that without entertaining activities available, the soldiers would cause trouble with town folks, or even among themselves. Off- duty boredom mixed with too much beer was not healthy or safe.

Out of that experience came the United Services Organization. When Marshall returned to Washington, he had a committee established to plan recreational activities for the army. There should be a place soldiers could go to relax, and find some decent entertainment of some kind. From his committee came a joint military-civilian business that eventually grew into the largest theatrical booking agency in the world. All the popular singing and comedy stars of the time including Al Jolson, Joe E. Brown, Red Skelton, Bob Hope, Bing Crosby, Dinah Shore, Marlene Dietrich, took their shows to the military bases all over the world for the USO.

In the smaller towns and cities near military bases, USO canteens provided places where soldiers could go to eat, play pool, ping pong, cards or Bingo, and dance to records. If the town had no movie theater, a projector, screen and rented films were often brought in, and the show began. The USO was worldwide and entertained millions.

Beginning in 1941, the women of America were working in full force to do their part for the war. By 1943, some five million women were working in the airplane factories or ammunition plants where their husbands or boyfriends would have been, had they not been drafted. While some went to work, about 65,000 others put on the uniform of the Women's Army Auxiliary Corps (WAAC).

General Marshall was in favor of having women in the Army even before they were authorized to be there. Women could do the jobs that some soldiers were doing, especially office work, telephone operators, drivers, and such. When he was leaving for the 1941 Thanksgiving weekend, he shook his finger at his Chief of Personnel, Major General John H. Hildring and said, "I want a Women's Corps right away and I don't want any excuses."

There were plenty of excuses, but none that lasted. Four days after Pearl Harbor the first legislation to establish a women's division of the Army was being formed. Congress had to approve a bill, which would allow women to be part of the armed forces, because it was such a new and controversial idea.

Mrs. Oveta Culp Hobby, a newspaper woman, whose husband was a former Texas governor, helped General Marshall advance the development of the WAAC by testifying in Congress, and helping him with the basic planning. There was plenty of opposition to the idea, but the two of them persevered.

Once the bill cleared Congress, General Marshall acted quickly. He appointed Mrs. Hobby to head the WAAC and on May 16, 1942, she was sworn in as the director. When her uniform arrived in June, General Marshall pinned the silver eagles of a colonel on for her. Congress had only allowed her to be paid what a major would earn, but Marshall assured them, that as the director she was doing a colonel's job and would be paid a colonel's salary. In June of 1943, Congress took the step that Marshall had favored all along. The word auxiliary was dropped from the term WAAC, and the Women's Army Corps, the WACs, were fully integrated into the U.S. Army.

The January 3, 1944 issue of TIME magazine carried George C. Marshall's picture on the front cover and named him their "Man of the Year" claiming, "Never in U.S. history has a military man enjoyed such respect on Capitol Hill."

But not everyone thought Marshall was always right. Somewhat similar to General Pershing, Chief of Staff George C. Marshall became known as "ruthless" in his removal of officers, even good friends, who were not doing their job to his satisfaction. He replaced older majors, colonels, and generals of many years with younger, more competent, and more aggressive ones. The President and Congress gave Marshall the power to do this by changing the outdated seniority rule, under which Marshall had endured.

Marshall often regretted having to retire his old friends from active service, but the war would required mental and physical strength, good health, determination, and fortitude of the highest caliber. He found that many of the National Guard officers did not meet the standards he had set for high commanding positions.

They too, were replaced. George C. Marshall lost some old friends and made some new enemies in doing what he thought was best for the entire U.S.Army, even if it hurt individual egos.

But on a personal level, his common touch was reflected in the uniform he wore as chief of staff—always plain and simple, with no fancy braid, medals or gadgets. He wore no medals, unless required, for he needed no reminders of who he was. His official car, that he was driven around Washington in, had no flags on it. He wanted, or seemed to need, no personal recognition—only simple order and efficiency. Yet, on the other hand, he was not as simple to get along with in the office.

Marshall was known for his tough demands for thorough and brief reports. Sometimes he demanded "on my desk in the morning" statistics, estimates, and figures that required his staff to stay at work all night to get them ready for his morning inspection. Then he would look at their red-rimmed eyes and say, "You look tired. Why don't you get more sleep?"

When Marshall went home to Quarters One in the evening, he was often exhausted, but restless. Sometimes he and Mrs. Marshall would walk along the Arlington, Virginia streets in the twilight and on into darkness as he talked through his problems. She said that he would talk and talk and talk, but she mainly listened without comment, because he did not need her response, just her presence.

She wrote, "It was as though he lived outside of himself and George Marshall was someone he was constantly appraising, advising and training to meet a situation." She heard him say, "I cannot afford the luxury of sentiment, mine must be cold logic," and "I cannot allow myself to get angry . . . it is too exhausting . . . My brain must be kept clear. . . "

His mind did stay clear and contained vast knowledge of the war problems and situations. He kept up with all the war fronts, knew what was happening in each area and how each part connected to the whole. He was always in close contact with President Roosevelt, senior generals and admirals, as well as the Allied military leaders. He was questioned often by the news media, because they knew he had the facts and figures they needed.

George C. Marshall was a master of the press conference. For him, a press conference was a gathering of news reporters from

magazines such as *Life, Time, Collier's,* and *The Saturday Evening Post* and major newspapers like *The Chicago Tribune, The New York Times,* and *The Washington Post,* as well as the national radio reporters from NBC, CBS, and ABC all asking questions. A news conference was time-consuming and could be tiresome. Reporters often asked the same thing more than once and the person being interviewed had to repeat answers already given because the reporters were not listening to each other.

One story of a Marshall news conference that took place in Algiers in May of 1943, after the Allies had won in North Africa, goes like this: To save time, General Marshall offered to answer one question for each reporter, and there were sixty reporters in the room. He heard each question in turn, all the way around the room. After the last question, he took a deep breath, looked off into space for about thirty seconds, then began to talk. He spoke for about forty minutes, and covered all the questions about the war. As he answered their one question, he looked directly at the person who had asked it. Everything fit together perfectly and in order. The reporters were astonished. His memory was amazing.

In March of 1942, George C. Marshall presented an idea to President Roosevelt that would help end the war. It was a simple idea: build a huge U.S. Army, send it to England, combine it with the British forces, cross the English Channel and invade France, and overcome the German army. The Allies could then free France and the rest of Western Europe from the Nazis. Roosevelt listened to the plan and liked it. He said that Marshall should present his idea to Sir Winston Churchill in London himself.

Marshall arrived in London in early April with his plan for a cross-channel crossing and an invasion of France to take place in 1943. Churchill seemed to like the plan, which had the code name Roundup, and Marshall thought he had accepted it. Marshall came back to Washington at the end of two weeks thinking Roundup would be accepted.

While her husband was in England, Katherine Marshall went to work on Dodona Manor, the house in Leesburg, Virginia they had bought the year before. The place was sturdy, but had been neglected and needed repairs. They had not yet lived in the house, but had spent a few weekends there. She planned to surprise him with her own clean-up and fix-up campaign battle against dirt and neglect. She hired bricklayers, painters, carpenters and yardmen to help her. A new garage was built to replace the old carriage house, brick sidewalks were laid leading from the house to the garden and the garage. Trees were trimmed, shrubs were pruned, and everything looked much better. She could hardly wait for him to see it.

General Marshall arrived at the airport, Mrs. Marshall greeted him and waited while he finished some paper work in his office, and then they drove out to Leesburg through the beautiful spring afternoon, arriving at Dodona Manor just at sunset. She wrote, "Then followed the happiest hours of the past three years. . . He stopped the car, got out and walked around, taking in every detail. Finally he turned and said in a husky voice, 'This is Home, a real home after forty-one years of wandering."

Katherine was afraid that George would be upset with the amount of money she had spent on the remodeling and fix-up of Dodona Manor. She reminded him that she knew he did not like it when job estimates went over budget, but that he must remember that it always costs more to do things fast. He laughed at that and assured her, he was so pleased with the house, her job would get no negative reviews. Whenever he could spare a day or two from the office, he went to Dodona and worked in his gardens.

The house was more of a success than Marshall's Roundup idea was. Prime Minister Churchill liked Marshall's plan, but not for 1943. What he wanted was an invasion of North Africa, and that is what happened. Operation Roundup did not happen, but turned into Operation Overlord, which did not take place until June of 1944.

The Overlord plan required a lot of planning and discussion. All in all, over the two years, there were 90 separate meetings on the subject of Overlord. The leaders of the three allied powers, Franklin D. Roosevelt, Britain's Sir Winston Churchill, and Joseph Stalin of the Soviet Union, met in Tehran, Iran in late November 1943. The hardest decision was: who would lead, who would direct the generals? Because the United States was contributing the largest number of men, Roosevelt was to choose the lead commander. Who would be the supreme commander of Overlord?

General Eisenhower and General Marshall discussing Overlord plan.

When General John J. Pershing heard that Roosevelt might be thinking of letting Marshall lead the troops into Overlord, he wrote to Roosevelt that Marshall was too valuable and was needed in Washington, that no one could replace him, that no one else could fill his shoes. Roosevelt answered General Pershing, letting him know he understood his position, but also saying that he wanted Marshall to have the chance to be "the Pershing of the Second World War."

George C. Marshall certainly wanted to be the leader of Overlord. After all, Operation Overlord was his idea, his plan. Who knew better than he how it should work? Many thought that President Roosevelt would choose Marshall as the Supreme Commander, and that he should. Many assumed that Marshall would claim the job for himself, and line up plenty of capable generals and colonels to help him. One possibility was to bring General Eisenhower to Washington, as chief of staff, and send George C. Marshall to England to lead Overlord.

After forty-two years of service, Marshall had never been on the front line of fire in war as a commanding general. Now was the time, if ever there was to be a time. Yet, he was sixty-three years old, and he had replaced several generals, younger than himself, with even younger generals. Regardless of his age, Marshall could have been a commanding general but nobody else could take his place as chief of staff in the middle of the war.

In December of 1943, Marshall and Roosevelt were in Cairo at meetings concerning the plans for Overlord. FDR was worried as to what to do about naming a supreme commander. Roosevelt felt that Europe was important, but Europe was only one war zone out of many around the world for the United States. The center of the whole war was in Washington, and the President needed George C. Marshall there more than Marshall needed to lead Overlord.

Marshall and Roosevelt met together alone, as they had four years earlier in Washington, when Marshall was selected to be chief of staff. Roosevelt asked Marshall in which position he felt he could be of the most service to the country. Marshall told Roosevelt that he, as Commander and Chief must be the one to decide, but that either way was all right with him. Marshall said that he would gladly do whatever the President wanted him to do.

General Marshall visits with General MacArthur in the Southwest
Pacific in December, 1943.

Roosevelt told Marshall, "I do not think I could sleep well at night with you out of the country." Therefore, George C. Marshall remained as chief of staff and, at Marshall's suggestion, Dwight D. Eisenhower was chosen to be the Supreme Commander of Operation Overlord. General Marshall was deeply disappointed, but he did not complain. His unspoken, personal wish had been to lead the Normandy Invasion, but his duty was to serve his country to the best of his ability. That he would do from his Pentagon office.

The morning after Roosevelt's decision, Marshall made a quiet and early exit by plane from Cairo. The Pacific areas of the war needed attention, also. He went to visit with General Douglas MacArthur, the Pacific forces commander, on his way back to his office in Washington. The Supreme Commander question was settled, the next question for George C. Marshall was: would Operation Overlord succeed?

General Omar Bradley, General Hap Arnold, Admiral Ernest King, General Dwight Eisenhower and General George C. Marshall discussing the outcome of D-Day.

Reporting for Duty

Chapter 14

Worldwide General

June 6, 1944 — August 14, 1945

The largest military land, sea, an air invasion in history, known worldwide as D-Day, took place on June 6, 1944 along the coast of Normandy, France. In the pre-dawn darkness, about 13,000 British and American paratroopers landed inland to secure roads and bridges, and gliders dropped important technical equipment. They were followed by 9,000 airplanes, 4,000 transport ships and 600 warships bringing 175,000 soldiers from Britain. As the troops came ashore, on five different beaches, they were met with the coastal artillery and gunfire of the German army. By the end of the day, the number of casualties (dead, wounded, or missing) totaled 9,500. The heroic Allied troops had landed.

The plans for Operation Overlord were made by General George C. Marshall, yet he had no hesitation in giving General Eisenhower the credit for making the plan work. It was under Eisenhower's command that all the other generals led their men. General Marshall later wrote to General Eisenhower: "You have completed your mission with the greatest victory in the history of warfare. You have commanded with outstanding success the most powerful military force that has ever been assembled . . . You have made history, great history for the good of all mankind and you have stood for all we hope for and admire in an officer of the United States Army."

The community of Bedford, Virginia with a population of 3,200 in 1944, has the national distinction of having the most citizen-soldiers killed on D-Day. The National Guard unit from Bedford, A Company of the 116th Infantry, 29th Division, lost nineteen men that day on Omaha Beach, with two others dying of their wounds a few days later. A National D-Day Memorial, honoring those men, and all others involved in the Normandy Invasion, is now located in Bedford and open to the public. President George W. Bush spoke at the memorial dedication ceremony on June 6, 2001.

General Marshall went to France for the first time since 1919, on June 8, 1944. General Hap Arnold and Admiral Ernest J. King went with him to personally congratulate General Omar Bradley, General Leonard T. Gerow, especially, for their commanding leadership at Omaha Beach on D-Day. The visiting leaders wanted to view the landing beaches and mingle with the men who had made the invasion—the Allied soldiers, sailors, airmen, and marines. They were able to visit with some of the wounded men, and they saw the temporary cemetery where today there is a permanent one. Sir Winston Churchill, and several of the British military leaders came from England, and they all met to eat together and discuss the success of Operation Overlord.

In December of 1944, Congress passed a bill creating the rank of 5-stars for General Marshall, along with Generals Eisenhower, Arnold, and MacArthur. For the Navy, Admirals Leahy, King, and Nimitz also received five-star status. Secretary of War Henry Stimson decided the proper title for the five Army generals would be General of the Army. General Marshall approved completely of that decision. Although Marshall did not feel the need for another star, he was more acceptant of the promotion idea in that way. Even if he did have only four stars, Geneal Pershing could remain the one and only General of the Armies.

After D-Day, it took another eleven months of fighting and many more Allied lives before the war in Europe was ended. Operation Overlord ended many lives, but it also marked the beginning of the end for the Nazis. The German Army began to crumble, even if slowly. In late April of 1945, Adolph Hitler committed suicide, and the German surrender came soon afterwards, on May 7, 1945. General Dwight D. Eisenhower accepted the unconditional surrender of the German military leaders at a school in Rheims, France.

On April 12, 1945, before Germany surrendered, Franklin D. Roosevelt died at his "Little White House" in Warm Springs, Georgia. Mrs. Roosevelt asked George C. Marshall to be in charge of the funeral arrangements, and later she wrote him a thank-you note to say, "My husband would have been grateful and I know it was all as he would have wished it. He always spoke of his trust in you and of his affection for you."

General Marshall always spoke to or of the only president to be elected to four terms as Mr. Roosevelt or Mr. President, but never Franklin or plain Roosevelt. During the years between 1942-45, Marshall and Roosevelt had grown in understanding of one another. They were not close friends, but they respected one another. The President had depended on Marshall for honest evaluations of the nation's wartime situation and advice on what to do next. Marshall depended on Roosevelt's support for his suggestions and decisions. They respected each other's special style in getting things done. Marshall was truly sorry that Roosevelt had not lived to hear of the Allied victory in Europe. Vice President Harry S. Truman became the 33rd U.S. president on April 12, 1945, following Roosevelt's death. He would see the war to its end.

It was on President Truman's 61st birthday when he announced that the war in Europe was finished. V-E (Victory in Europe) Day was celebrated in America, with joy and sadness. The celebration was welcome, but it was limited, because America was still fighting to defeat Japan. People were thankful and hopeful. It would not be long now until WW II was successfully concluded. At noon on V-E Day, the secretary of war, Henry Stimson sent word for George C. Marshall to come to his office.

General Marshall found fourteen generals and high officials sitting in a semi-circle around the large desk with an empty chair in the center. Stimson asked Marshall to sit down, and then he made a short speech, beginning with, "I want to acknowledge my great personal debt to you, Sir, in common with the whole country." He complimented Marshall for his unselfish work as chief of staff and for not taking the command of Overlord and said, "I have seen a great many soldiers in my lifetime and you, Sir, are the finest soldier I have ever known." The Secretary of War had paid the Army Chief of Staff a sincere compliment.

Katherine Marshall wrote, "When George returned home that evening he was strangely silent. He made no mention of what had occurred in the Secretary's Office," and she knew nothing of it until the next morning when she received copies of Stimson's remarks from Colonel Frank McCarthy. Then she ". . . knew why my husband had been so silent. . . His feelings were too deep for words. His gratitude could not be expressed."

At that time, the war news reached the people by way of radio, not television, and newsreels shown at the movie houses. Newsreels were shown after the previews and cartoons and just before the main feature. Soon after V-E Day, a 20-minute film called "Two Down and One to Go" came out in theaters across the nation. George C. Marshall had the film made to inform the public about the reasons for Operation Overlord, and he talked about what was happening around the world and how The War was really one war, not two. He introduced the commanding generals of the Army and the Air Corps, and they talked about their different assignments. In this way, the film was informative and of great value to millions of Americans.

President Truman learned, a few minutes after he was sworn in, of the secret weapon that was being developed in laboratories and was to be tested in the desert near Alamogordo, New Mexico. During the past few years, the War Department, directed mainly by Secretary Stimson and George C. Marshall, had been planning and developing the Manhatten Project, an atomic bomb, the most powerful weapon ever created. In late 1944, Marshall was told the A-bomb would be ready for use in eight months.

The war in the Pacific seemed constant. So many people killed or taken prisoner. Marshall was afraid that if the United States was forced to attack Japan, as they had done Germany on D-Day, the loss of American lives would run into the hundreds of thousands of lives. He and Henry Stimson suggested to President Truman that the first bomb should be dropped on a military target. If that did not cause Japan's surrender, then a second one would be dropped on an important manufacturing center. He hoped the civilians would be warned in time to leave either area. No one really knew how massive the destruction would be. Two atomic bombs, one on August 6 and the second on August 9, 1945, were dropped on two major cities of Japan, Hiroshima and Nagasaki.

The Japanese officially surrendered on August 14, and the formal surrender to the United States of America came on September 2, 1945. General Douglas MacArthur, the Supreme Commander of

Allied Forces in the Pacific, accepted the Japanese surrender on board the U.S. battleship *Missouri* in Tokyo Bay. The second Great War of the Twentieth Century had at last ended.

With Japan's defeat, the celebrations began in earnest. American people everywhere celebrated in the streets and towns, their homes and churches. Horns, sirens, and bells sounded across the land. August 14, 1945 was named V-J Day, meaning Victory over Japan had been won. Three months after the Japanese surrender the Second World War ended. When Marshall officially retired from the U.S.Army, President Harry S. Truman said, "In a war unparalleled in magnitude and horror, millions of Americans gave their country outstanding service, General of the Army George C. Marshall gave it victory."

Just as the nation's people felt relief from duty on the battle-front, or the home front of the war, George C. Marshall felt relieved of his duty, too. He wanted to retire, but he wanted to talk to the president, before he sent in his letter or resignation. He wanted to help Harry Truman appoint a new chief of staff. Every evening Katherine would ask, "Did you talk to him today?" and George would say "No, not today." The President was always too busy. He guessed he would have to write a letter, after all.

Marshall was tired, not just in body, but mentally and emotion-ally. He was at the end of his sixth year as chief of staff, when nor-mally a general would serve four years. He had done his job well, but the war years had taken a great toll on his health and energy. He was after all, sixty-five years old. It was time to leave his office at the Pentagon. His job was done, at last. It was time, he thought, to go home and rest.

Generals Marshall and Arnold went pheasant hunting, November 24, 1945.

Reporting for Duty

Chapter 15

At Ease, By George!

November 1945

In August of 1945, while the country was celebrating the end of World War II, General George C. Marshall wrote a letter to President Harry S. Truman, stating his wish to retire. At home, George and Katherine began to plan their own kind of celebration. They dragged out the maps again. These were not maps of war zones or army bases, but of lovely and remote vacation spots and new roads to explore by car. Mrs. Marshall said that although their hair was gray, there was nothing gray in their plans.

In addition to Dodona Manor, they had bought a second retirement home in Pinehurst, North Carolina. They would spend part of their winters there and their summers at Dodona Manor in Leesburg. General Marshall was ready to spend time working in his garden during the spring and summer and quail hunting in the fall. Maybe they would spend some time near the Gulf of Mexico during the coldest weather, where they both could do some serious fishing. They could have an early spring in Pinehurst and a late one in Leesburg. Actually, they were planning a honeymoon.

When they married in 1930, they "stepped from the altar into Army activities," Mrs. Marshall said, and had been following Army routines all fifteen years. They were due some time just for themselves. They made their plans with excitement, and were surprised they both felt ready to move on with their private lives. They began packing their things into boxes and prepared to leave Fort Myer, Quarters I. That was not as easy or as much fun as planning their retirement trips.

Moving out of Quarters 1 would take a bit doing, but they would do it slowly, one car full at a time. The General had a large

President Truman congratulates General George C. Marshall at his
retirement ceremony.

assortment of Army clothes; clothes for all climates from the Arctic to the tropics, full dress uniforms to everyday khakis. There were bedrolls and mess kits, hats and caps, and boxes and boxes of books and reports. Souvenirs sent to them, and to him, from all over the world by friends and fans filled other closets. They even had chickens to move, or leave!

One day back in the Spring, Mrs. Marshall had called their grocer and asked if he had any "fresh chickens." She was slightly surprised when he sent them 100 baby Plymouth Rock chicks, and she was even more surprised they had kept them! They raised them in the basement for the first three weeks, then had a pen built in the back yard. As the chickens grew, they took up more space, and so to make room, their cook killed and cooked some every few days. The Marshalls ate a lot of "fresh chicken."

By August, they had twenty-four large chickens, and they decided not move to them. They left them at Quarters One for General Eisenhower, the new chief of staff. Surely, he and Mrs. Eisenhower could use some good, "fresh chickens", too .

Following Marshall's suggestion, General Dwight David Eisenhower had been selected by President Truman to replace General Marshall. Marshall was pleased to issue the official Army orders that would bring Eisenhower home from Europe. Once the decision was made, "a great load seemed to roll off my husband's shoulders. At breakfast he was carefree, the heavy lines between his eyes began to disappear, he laughed once more," Mrs. Marshall wrote. They happily watched the trucks loaded with their belongings leave Quarters I and head toward Leesburg, and without any chickens.

The fall of 1945 seemed especially lovely to the Marshalls as they moved from one house to another. Daily, Marshall went to the Pentagon office to finish his work, and Katherine went to Dodona Manor to see to the unloading and putting away of their things. After work, he came to Leesburg to help her, and they returned to Ft. Myer the next morning. They repeated the process until their move was finished. After moving out of Quarters 1, they spent several days in an apartment at Fort Myer Officers Club so that Marshall could work in his office while waiting for General Eisenhower to arrive. The seasons were changing in an orderly fashion, and so were they.

In addition to moving his personal belongings from the Pentagon, Marshall needed to help disassemble the army. Taking the Army apart after the war, took almost as much work as putting it together before the war. General Marshall went to Congress again. This time he talked about demobilization — the process of bringing soldiers home, discharging, and dismissing most of the 8,000,000 Army and Air Corps men and women. Discharging the soldiers from the army, in orderly fashion, was almost as hard as getting them drafted, enlisted and trained for battle. Once again he came up with a plan.

George C. Marshall designed a point system, depending on how long and where a person had served. A soldier with 85 points was eligible for immediate discharge. The ones with the hardest tours of duty and with waiting families were being sent home first. Sometimes records were mixed up and men were unhappy.

Once as the Marshalls were traveling from Fort Myer to Leesburg, driving in their private car, they picked up a hitch hiking soldier. The General was wearing his casual civilian clothes, instead of his uniform. The point system of discharge had recently started, and the soldier began to talk about it. He had been over-seas and had taken part in many battles. General Marshall said that in such a case, he was eligible for an immediate discharge. The soldier said he didn't stand a chance of that happening.

"But you are bound to have enough points," Marshall said.

The soldier almost yelled, "Points! That stuff is all hooey. You have got to have a wife and children."

"What do you mean all hooey? The War Department announced that if you have as much service time as you have, and have fought the battles that you have fought, you can get your dis-charge," Marshall told him.

The soldier answered, "That's what you think. But it doesn't work that way. I have to have a wife and children or it's no go."

And so they argued back and forth as they rode along to Leesburg. Marshall added up the man's points for him, and still the fellow did not believe it. "That's just what the Brass Hats tell you. It's all hooey. Who do you think you are, General Marshall?" the soldier asked.

When he heard that yes, he was General Marshall and, "What is your name and outfit? You'll be out of the Army tomorrow, " the hitch hiker was speechless.

In November of 1945, General of the Army George C. Marshall was relieved, as Chief of Staff, by General of the Army Dwight David Eisenhower. His retirement day was set as November 18, 1945. On November 26, General Marshall was awarded an Oak Leaf Cluster to be added to his Distinguished Service Medal. The presentation was made by President Harry S. Truman.

Part of the citation that President Truman read aloud, says: "His standards of character, conduct and efficiency inspired the entire Army, the Nation and the world. To him, as much as to any individual the United States owes its future. He takes his place at the head of the great commanders of history."

Other comments worth remembering about General Marshall include: Sir Winston Churchill called Marshall "the organizer of victory," and also said, "Succeeding generations must not be allowed to forget his achievements and his example." General Eisenhower referred to George C. Marshall as, "the strongest weapon I have always had in my hand."

On the day, they left Fort Myer for the last time they picked up no hitchhikers along the way to Leesburg. They were going home. After preparing Dodona Manor for the winter, they planned to go to Pinehurst, North Carolina for the winter at their cottage, named Liscomb Lodge. George could do some quail shooting and maybe play a bit of golf. Perhaps they would head for the Gulf of Mexico in January for some beaches and fishing. Whatever they did or wherever they went, they would come back to Dodona in the springtime to plant a new garden. They were retired and could do what they pleased whenever it pleased them.

Katherine Marshall wrote, "When we got out (of the car) we stood for a few minutes on the portico. The sun was shining through the trees, the surroundings were beautifully peaceful. It all seemed a good omen." George C. Marshall had lived in twenty different places during his forty-three years of army service. He was home to stay, at last.

"We entered the house and I started up the front stairs to go to my room for a little rest before dinner. Halfway up I heard the telephone ring. George went back to answer it," Mrs. Marshall said.

An hour later, when she came down, Katherine found General Marshall in a reclining chair, resting. The radio was broadcasting the three o'clock news. "President Truman has appointed General of the Army George C. Marshall as his Special Ambassadorial Envoy to China. He will leave immediately," the announcer said.

General Marshall stood up and went toward Katherine. "That phone call as we came in was from the President. I could not bear to tell you until you had had your rest."

President Truman needed George C. Marshall's help again, and Marshall could not turn down a chance to serve his country.

Although the storms were over, and the sun had come out, the pot of gold at the end of the rainbow was still out of reach. His retirement was postponed, and a few weeks later he left for China. He would perform crucial public jobs for six more years before he could finally retire and be fully at ease, by George.

Sir Winston Churchill said about George C. Marshall, "In war he was as wise and understanding in counsel as he was resolute in action . . . . succeeding generations must not be allowed to forget his achievements or his example."

General and Mrs. Marshall, 1945

A Letter from General Marshall

Lillian Craig was a teacher in Roanoke, Virginia. She considered her nine to twelve year-old students as normal and healthy. Their main problem had to do with reading. She told them about George C. Marshall and they had questions they wanted to ask him. With her help, they wrote a letter to General Marshall. They asked what sort of boy he had been and if he could suggest what they could do to help win the war. This is part of his letter to them and is dated March 15, 1944.

"You ask what kind of boy I was. I am afraid I cannot give you a proper estimate because I could not see myself as others saw me . . . I will tell you this, that I was a poor student and I was anything but a success in my particular world. Fortunately, while I was still in my teens I realized some of my deficiencies and made a tremendous effort to correct them. A good bit of this reform was due to the example of others and the leadership of some of my teachers . . . They caught me just in time.

"You ask what I suggest that you should do to help win the war . . . I hesitate to answer because I know it will be depressing to you to be told to work hard and do well all the small tasks you are called on to perform. However, these are the basis of discipline, and discipline is vital to a soldier and to success in battle, and self-discipline is probably one of the very important factors in the life of a man or woman. What you do today is of tremendous importance in what you will do tomorrow . . .

"If the world observes that all our young people have turned to every task with an intensity of purpose to make themselves better citizens, the world will be greatly impressed with the power of this country. Because that power is determined by its citizens, by their good sense, their integrity, their willingness to do their duty as citizens. By such conduct on your part, you will discourage our enemies and encourage our friends and those who are 'on the fence' trying to decide with whom they should align themselves."

Faithfully yours,

George C. Marshall

General Marshall waves to the crowd in a Philadelphia parade
November 13, 1945.

162

*"Succeeding generations must not be allowed to forget his achievements
and his example." Sir Winston Churchill*   (Dick Skutt photo)

The Marshall Statue

In 1977, VMI's Superintendent, Lieutenant General Richard L. Irby, class of 1939, recommended, and the Board of Visitors approved that a statue should be made of General George C. Marshall. The VMI Foundation and its chairman, General Lemuel C. Shepherd, Jr. '27, USMC (Retired) agreed to raise the funds to pay for the statue. In planning the fund-raising campaign, Mr. Joseph D. Neikirk, class of '32, went to his Brother Rat, Adolfo (Pilo) Ponzanelli. In turn, Mr. Ponzanelli, the first Mexican graduate of VMI and a marble industrialist in Mexico, enlisted his close friend, a famous sculptor, Augusto Bozzano, a native of Italy who also lived in Mexico. Together they planned and created the statue. General Marshall's uniforms, insignia, and such were sent to Mexico by the Marshall Library officials to help the sculptor achieve accuracy. The the seven-foot bronze statue shows General Marshall at the age of sixty-four, wearing his World War II uniform. His five star emblem is shown on the statue base, cut from Santo Tomas marble and provided by Pilo Ponzanelli. Two 28-inch miniature duplicates of the statue, also made by Bozzano, were given to the VMI Museum and to the George C. Marshall Museum.

On VMI's Founder's Day, November 11th, in 1978, the statute of General of the Army George C. Marshall was officially dedicated. Brigadier general Frank McCarthy, class of '33, who worked closely with General Marshall during World War II, made the dedication address.

In closing he said, "I think that the General, on his pre-war horseback rides from Ft. Myer around the perimeter of Arlington National Cemetery, may have read the inscription at the base of the Monument to the Conferderate Soldier, sculptured by another VMI graduate, Moses Ezekial: 'Not for fame or reward, Not for place or rank, Not lured by ambition, Or goaded by necessity, But in simple obedience to duty as he understood it...' I hope he read it, for it applies so precisely to General Marshall."

The statue is a symbolic reminder to all cadets, and an introduction to VMI visitors, of General George C. Marshall, class of 1901, of his life and contributions to our country's history.

(Both The VMI Museum and the VMI Archives provided some of the above information.

U.S. Army Service Record of George C. Marshall

February 2, 1902 — Commissioned second lieutenant of Infantry, U.S. Army—Uniontown, Pa.

May 1902- November 1903 — Duty in the Philippines

December 1903 - August 1906 — Duty at Fort Reno, Oklahoma

August 1906 –June 1908 — Student, Army Infantry and Cavalry School and Staff College, Fort Leavenworth

August 1908 –June 1910 — Instructor, Army Services Schools, Fort Leavenworth, Kansas

March 7, 1907 — Promoted to first lieutenant

June 1908 — Appointed instructor, Army Service Schools and Staff College

June 1911 — Inspector-instructor, Massachusetts Volunteer Militia, Boston

September 1912-June 1913—Duty with Fourth Infantry Regiment, Fort Logan Roots, Arkansas; Fort Snelling Minnesota; Texas City, Texas.

August 1913—May 1916 Duty in the Philippines; aide de campe to Major General Hunter Liggett

July 1916 — Appointed aide de camp to Major General J. Franklin Bell, San Francisco

July 1, 1916 — Promoted to captain

June 1917 — November 1918 — Duty with AEF (American Expeditionary Force); France; assistant chief of staff, G-3, First Division; G-3, GHQ; assistant chief of staff, First Army; G-3 temporary promotions to major, lieutenant colonel, and colonel.

November 1918—April 1919 Armistice; chief of staff, Eighth Corps; G-3 duty, GHQ, AEF, France

May 1919 — Appointed aide de camp to General John J. Pershing, France and Washington, D.C.

July 1, 1920 — Promoted to major (permanent), Regular Army

August 21, 1923 — Promoted to lieutenant colonel, Regular Army

September 1924 -May 1927- Duty with Fifteenth Infantry Regiment, Tientsin, China.

July 1927 — Duty as Instructor, Army War College, Washington, D.C.

October 1927 — Appointed assistant commandant, Infantry School, Fort Benning, Georgia.

June 1932 — Appointed commander, Fort Screven, Georgia,

June 1933 — Appointed commander, Fort Moultrie, South Carolina

September 1, 1933 — Promoted to colonel, Regular Army

October 1933 — Appointed senior instructor, Illinois National Guard, Chicago, Illinois

October 1, 1936 — Promoted to brigadier general, Regular Army appointed commander, 5th Brigade of 3rd Division, Vancouver Barracks, Washington

September 1, 1939 - Promotion to permanent major general and general (temporary)

December 16, 1944 — Appointed General of the Army, (temporary) with 5 stars

April 11, 1946 — Appointed General of the Army (permanent)

February 28, 1947 —Retired from active service in U.S.Army

March 1, 1949 — Restored to the Active list

Military Decorations and Awards of George C. Marshall

United States:
Distinguished Service Medal with First Oak Leaf Cluster
Silver Star
Gold Medal expressing "Thanks of Congress"
Philippine Campaign Medal
Mexican Border Service Medal
World War I Victory Medal with four battle clasps
Army of Occupation of Germany Medal
American Defense Service Medal with Foreign Service Clasp
American Campaign Medal
Asiatic-Pacific Campaign Medal
European-African-Middle Eastern Campaign Medal with two
  bronze service stars
World War II Victory Medal
National Defense Service Medal
Foreign:
Brazil — Order of Military Merit, Grade of Grand Officer
Chile —— Order del Merito
Columbia — Grand Cross of the Order of Boyaco
Cuba — Order of Military Merit, First Class
Ecuador — Star of Abdon Calderon, First Class
France — Legion of Honor, degree of Officer (1919); promoted to
  degree of Grand Croix (1945)
Great Britain — Knight Grand Cross, Order of Bath (Mlitary
  Division)
Greece — Grand Cross, with Swords, of the Royal Order of George I
Italy — Order of the Crown of Italy, Grade of Officer; Order of
  Saints Maurice and Lazarus, Grade of Officer
Liberia — Centennial Medal
Montenegro — Silver Medal for Bravery
Morocco — Grand Cross of Ouissam Alaouite Cherifien
Netherlands — Knight of the Grand Cross with Swords in the Order
  of Orange Nassau
Panama — Medal of La Solidaridad, Second Class
Peru — Gran Oficial de Sol de Peru
U.S.S.R. Order of Suvarov, First DegreeCivilian Awards (19021-
  1945)
Theodore Roosevelt Distinguished Service Medal of Honor, 1945
Honorary Degrees
Command and General Staff School, 1934
Washington and Jefferson College, 1939
Pennsylvania Military College, 1940
College of William and Mary, 1941
Trinity College, 1941
Norwich University, 1942

Some Army Terms

Allied Forces, allies —-the combined armed forces of countries fighting with the United States against the Central Powers (World War I) and the Axis (World War II).

Battalion — a military unit that includes a commander, his or her staff headquarters and three or four companies.

Brigade. A brigade consists of a commander, headquarters staff and normally three battalions.

Company — A small unit within a regiment. The company is commanded by a captain.

Corps — (core) a group of cadet companies, as the VMI Corps of Cadets, a group of civilians, as the Civilian Conservation Corps, a group of army divisions, or a special unit such as the Army Air Corps

Division — a group of battalions with a major general as commander

Front-line — the main line of defense, where the fighting is heaviest, where the two enemies meet , where combat takes place.

General — General is the highest Army officer rank and there are five levels of general, i.e., Brigadier General (1 star), Lieutenant General (2 stars), Major General (3 stars) General (4 stars) and General of the Army (5 stars)

Platoon — a smaller group within a military company, divided into squads or sections, and usually commanded by a lieutenant.

Rank — the level of an officer's position. George Marshall held the highest rank of any cadet during his final year at VMI, and the highest Army rank as Chief of Staff, 1939-45. Your army job depends on your rank. A general has the highest rank, and a private has the lowest.

Regiment — Soldiers affiliated with a regiment wear distinctive unit insignia and are associated with the same regiment throughout their army career.